The First
European Elections

Westview Replica Editions

The concept of Westview Replica Editions is a response to the continuing crisis in academic and informational publishing. Library budgets for books have been severely curtailed. Ever larger portions of general library budgets are being diverted from the purchase of books and used for data banks, computers, micromedia, and other methods of information retrieval. Interlibrary loan structures further reduce the edition sizes required to satisfy the needs of the scholarly community. Economic pressures on the university presses and the few private scholarly publishing companies have severely limited the capacity of the industry to properly serve the academic and research communities. As a result, many manuscripts dealing with important subjects, often representing the highest level of scholarship, are no longer economically viable publishing projects--or, if accepted for publication, are typically subject to lead times ranging from one to three years.

Westview Replica Editions are our practical solution to the problem. We accept a manuscript in camera-ready form, typed according to our specifications, and move it immediately into the production process. As always, the selection criteria include the importance of the subject, the work's contribution to scholarship, and its insight, originality of thought, and excellence of exposition. The responsibility for editing and proofreading lies with the author or sponsoring institution. We prepare chapter headings and display pages, file for copyright, and obtain Library of Congress Cataloging in Publication Data. A detailed manual contains simple instructions for preparing the final typescript, and our editorial staff is always available to answer questions.

The end result is a book printed on acid-free paper and bound in sturdy library-quality soft covers. We manufacture these books ourselves using equipment that does not require a lengthy make-ready process and that allows us to publish first editions of 300 to 600 copies and to reprint even smaller quantities as needed. Thus, we can produce Replica Editions quickly and can keep even very specialized books in print as long as there is a demand for them.

About the Book and Author

The First European Elections:
Neo-Functionalism and the European Parliament
Jane P. Sweeney

The first direct election of the European Parliament in 1979 was hailed as an event that would bring new momentum to the process of building a united Europe. That the first election did not have the expected outcome, argues the author of this book, can be attributed to flaws in the "Community method," which reflects the EEC's reliance on neo-functionalism. Dr. Sweeney investigates her hypothesis through a study of the 1979 electoral campaigns of the West German SPD, French Parti Socialiste, and British Labour Party, emphasizing the question of transnational cooperation among these members of the Confederation of Socialist Parties of the European Community. Her discussion of the Confederation's attempt to organize a united campaign among its nine constituent parties is based on extensive research on the workings of Parliament's political groups and on interviews and field work conducted before and after the June 1979 elections.

With the second direct election due to take place in 1984, the European Parliament's powers have not expanded, and once again there is concern about how to interest the public and the parties in the elected Parliament. Dr. Sweeney concludes that the present structure of the EEC is an impediment to political integration and suggests that national parties and European citizens will become concerned only when the Parliament has the power to make decisions that affect them.

Dr. Sweeney is an assistant professor of political science at St. John's University, New York.

Published in cooperation with the
Commission of the European Communities

The First
European Elections
Neo-Functionalism
and the European Parliament

Jane P. Sweeney

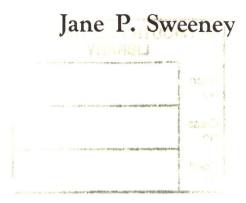

Westview Press / Boulder, Colorado

A Westview Replica Edition

Copyright © 1984 by Westview Press, Inc.

Published in 1984 in the United States of America by
    Westview Press, Inc.
    5500 Central Avenue
    Boulder, Colorado 80301
    Frederick A. Praeger, President and Publisher

Library of Congress Catalog Card Number: 83-51101
ISBN 0-86531-815-8

Printed and bound in the United States of America

10 9 8 7 6 5 4 3 2 1

To my parents,
Robert and Doris Sweeney,
whose concern about the role of politics
in securing the rights of ordinary people
has become mine

Contents

ix

Preface

"The voice of the spirit of Europe" is the European Commission's description of the Community's 434
member Parliament. Four years after the European Parliament's historic first direct election by the citizens
of nine countries, that voice is barely audible and one
must pause to wonder whether the spirit is equally weak.
The European Parliament is potentially one of the most
interesting legislative bodies in the world because of
the circumstances which created it, its unique transnational composition, and the power it may some day
wield. However, the gap between the real and the possible is very large indeed.

This study, begun as my doctoral dissertation, is
essentially two things at once: an investigation of neo-
functionalist integration theory on which the European
Community was premised, and an account of the roles of
three political parties in the first European elections
of June 1979. The direct election of the Parliament, an
important event for the Community in itself, is used
here as a vehicle for examining the dynamics of political integration. Specifically, I am interested in the
role of the electoral process in strengthening transnational bonds within the European Community.

Chapter One explores neo-functionalist theory in
some depth. While this theory is now passé and its
chief proponents have gone off to other intellectual
endeavors, it is important to recall that it is the
method of integration set into motion by the Treaty of
Rome which created the European Community on January 1,
1958. That is, while scholars today are not advocating
a neo-functionalist approach to integrating a region,
this continues to be the "Community method." Hence, it
is necessary to return to the theory and to try to establish where its flaws lie, to attempt to discover if
the method itself is responsible for the stagnation of
political integration among the member states.

The second direct election will take place in June
1984, and as of now it seems that it will be a less ex-

citing re-run of the first. The Parliament has not, on the strength of the prestige it was hoped would flow from democratic legitimacy, been able to expand its legal competence. True, the directly elected Members of the European Parliament (MEPs) have been more conscious of their prerogatives and more willing to challenge Council and Commission than were the former appointed MEPs, but their skirmishes have led to little in the way of concrete results. An example: as of summer 1983 it was expected that in the next few months Parliament would exercise its power to dismiss the entire fourteen member Commission of the European Communities. Why? Not to protest any particular action on the Commission's part, but to raise Parliament's profile as a hedge against expected voter apathy in the 1984 election.

While the Treaty of Rome calls for the establishment of a uniform electoral system, the 1984 election, like the first, will use ten national systems (Greece, which joined the Community in 1981, did not participate in the first direct election). Parliament devised and presented to the European Council a uniform system, but it was rejected. Such is the frustration of this legislative body as long as the Council is accountable to national governments and not to it.

In 1979 much of the "campaigning" was actually an informational get-out-the-vote drive financed by the Commission. While parties certainly developed election manifestos and campaigned with varying degrees of enthusiasm, they could not claim to voters that they could deliver on their electoral promises if victorious. The same will be true in 1984 unless some significant event occurs within the next few months. In the final chapter I suggest one possible situation which, were it to develop, might make the Parliament important to voters and national parties.

What has changed significantly since 1979 is the political position of each of the three parties studied here. The French Parti Socialiste has attained, through victory in the 1981 presidential election, a long desired legitimacy. Much of their effort in the 1979 Euro-campaign can be interpreted as part of a plan to enhance their image. Do they need to run so hard in 1984? The West German Social Democrats, who have dominated the Socialist Group of the Parliament in recent years, lost significant strength in their 1983 national elections, and must turn the tide in the 1984 European contest if they are to retain their thirty-five person bloc in the Socialist Group. In the United Kingdom, 1983 results were disastrous for the Labour Party, which was also humiliated in the 1979 European election. Pivotal for the socialists in general will be the roles played by the Greens in West Germany, the Social Democratic-Liberal Alliance in Britain, the Italian Socialist Party which has been gaining strength nationally,

and the Pan-Hellenic Socialist Union (PASOK) in Greece.
That is, while the 1984 elections will be structurally
similar to 1979, the politics affecting the transnational campaigns have changed significantly in key member
states. In general, Socialist Group solidarity will be
even more difficult to achieve.

The first European elections may be examined in
several ways. One may evaluate such data as who won or
lost, which polities evidenced interest through high
voter turnout, and which political groupings showed the
most strength across Europe. While knowledge such as
this is useful, it is also particular to June 1979.
There are ample reasons to expect considerably different
results in 1984. However, one can also view the first
direct elections in the context of the theory on which
the Community is premised, and search for clues about
the long term success of its goal of building a "new political community." This is far riskier than neatly
citing results and then going home, but it is hopefully
more profitable. For those who see the European Community as one of the most exciting entities in the contemporary world - and I must count myself in that group -
it is necessary to critically examine its successes and
failures. Here, I argue that the lack of democracy in
its structure is a significant weakness, and is in fact
the reason why individuals have not learned to relate
to it. That is, the method adopted in 1958 expects
people to develop an interest in and loyalty to an institution far removed from their lives and their control.

Many may disagree with my analysis and my solutions, as I disagree with the neo-functionalist method.
Perhaps if they do, they will be disposed to see in this
study a catalyst for their own thoughts. One day, all
of our efforts may add up to produce the full flowering
of "l'Europe des citoyens."

Jane P. Sweeney

Acknowledgments

The Commission of the European Communities awarded me a grant which partially subsidized publication of this volume. I am grateful for the Commission's decision, and must note that it is the most recent event in a long and fruitful relationship with the European Community's research librarians, European Parliamentarians, and members of the Parliament's Secretariat. The Community has provided me with unfailing access and cooperation.

Professor Adamantia Pollis of the New School for Social Research supervised this work at the dissertation stage, and has provided helpful advice and criticism since then. While she does not agree with all of my conclusions, discussion with her was a critical part of refining my ideas. Professors Neale Ronning and the late Saul Padover and Victor Baras of the New School were also most helpful. My former colleagues, Michael Suleiman at Kansas State University and John DeBrizzi at St. John's University, are thanked for encouraging me to seek publication.

Support for my field work in Europe was provided by the New School for Social Research. In addition to financial help, this "University in Exile" gave me a unique intellectual forum in which to dwell on the political future of Europe. The New School's Graduate Faculty went through a major internal crisis while I was there. Its future was secured through active participation of students and faculty who believed intently that people's lives should not be controlled by an unaccountable bureaucracy. The lesson was not lost to me as I pondered the implications of Parliament's minor role in the European Community system.

Friends and family who helped and humored me are sincerely thanked. Elaine Parker and Fran Sullivan gave significant editorial assistance. Particular appreciation goes to my mother, Doris Sweeney, who typed several drafts of this manuscript, correcting my spelling along the way. Though she nagged about her strong preference that I instead write a historical novel with a romantic subplot, she graciously accepted my disinclination to do so. For loyalty even one's child should not expect, she has my special thanks.

Lynne C. Rienner and Dean Birkenkamp of Westview Press, William Steerman and Victor Robinson of the New School, Vivien Jennings, Edith Magdalen Visoc, Mary Nelson, Lea Rissner, Gail Mansouri, and my students at KSU and St. John's all played important roles in this project. Linda Herbst, Barbara Roberson, Wilhelm Hennis, Lord Wayland Kennet, and Jan Kurleman were instrumental in my field work.

Jane P. Sweeney

Introduction

On November 14, 1978 <u>les</u> <u>Mineurs</u> <u>de</u> <u>fer</u> <u>de</u> <u>Lorraine</u>
staged a demonstration against economic policies which
they believed were threatening their job security. This
type of activity is usual among western labor unions and
certainly a chief <u>modus</u> <u>operandi</u> of the French Confédér-
ation Générale du <u>Travail</u> (CGT) to which these workers
belonged. What is unique about this particular demonstration is that it took place, not outside the National
Assembly in Paris, but on the steps of the Palais de
l'Europe in Strasbourg.[1] The miners were addressing
their demands, not to the government of France, but to
the European Community whose Parliament was in session
inside the Palais. Members of the European Parliament
(MEPs), when questioned about the leafleting union members, responded that this was the first time they remembered any European interest group demonstrating at a
parliamentary sitting.[2]

In speculating about why these miners went to
Strasbourg, several questions emerge: was their presence
a sign of growing perceptions on the part of Europeans
that the Community is increasingly an institution whose
decisions affect their lives? If so, were they correct
in acting analogously to their political behavior on the
national level, that is, pressuring the members of the
"legislature"? Is the European Parliament as consti-
tuted competent to process the demands of these workers?
And central to this study, if the Parliament can in fact
do little to affect the lives of individual Europeans,
will groups from the ten member countries ever organize
themselves in such a manner as to attempt to influence
the deliberations of this assembly?

These questions about the position of the European
Parliament in the political life of an integrated Europe
became particularly germane as the Community's political
parties prepared for the first direct elections to the
European Parliament, held throughout the member countries on June 7 and 10, 1979. Perceptions about the
effect of these elections on the process which has come

1

to be called "building Europe" differ considerably, but observers tend to agree that the direct elections were a momentous occasion for the Community.[3]

Any study of these elections must be built upon both theoretical and historical foundations. It is necessary to recall exactly what the European Community is trying to accomplish politically and to connect this goal with a body of theoretical work which tries to both explain about and advise the actors in the integration project. Having briefly considered Community goals and theorists, it will be possible to clearly state the parameters of this particular study.

The relationship between attempts by academics to build a cogent theory of regional integration and attempts by Europeans to build a regional system is very close. On the one hand, as Charles Pentland has observed, the Treaty of Rome which created the European Economic Community in January 1958 also created a laboratory in which neo-functionalist theorists could extensively investigate just how their idealized constructs would work in the real world.[4] Because they have often failed to work, neo-functionalism has been constantly developing and shifting its emphasis over last twenty-five years.[5] At the same time, though other theories have attempted to explain and influence European integration, over the course of time "neo-functionalism assumed the status of an unofficial ideology in Brussels."[6] The neo-functionalists (Ernst Haas, Leon Lindberg, Stuart Scheingold, Philippe Schmitter, and J.S. Nye are the major contributors to this body of theory) have relied extensively on the Community, while the Europeans have depended on these academics to point the way.

Where are they going? Perhaps the most incredible and exciting aspect of the Community project is that no one is quite sure. They are trying, according to Ernst Haas' earliest formulations, to build a "political community." Haas defines this pivotal term in The Uniting of Europe:

> Political community, therefore, is a condition in which specific groups and individuals show more loyalty to their central political institutions than to any other political authority, in a specific period of time and in a definable geographic space. In this study, this condition will be the one toward which the process of political integration is supposed to lead.[7]

Integration is the other central term, and we will once again use the Haas definition:

> Political integration is the process whereby

political actors in several distinct national
settings are persuaded to shift their loyalities,
expectations and political activities toward a
new centre, whose institutions possess or demand
jurisdiction over the pre-existing national state.[8]

Though there are discernable strands of divergence
among the theorists and the "Europeans," there is general agreement that the work of integration is the
gradual shift of elite expectations to a focus on the
institutions of the Community, and that when that shift
has reached some as yet undefined level a new political
community will have developed. A central problem of
this kind of ad hoc theorizing and institution building
is that it is difficult to develop proper strategies to
lead to an end point which no one is willing to define
in explicit and institutional terms. Additionally, it is
possible that the stagnation some observers see in the
recent history of the Community is due to incorrect
emphasis and misplaced analogies in the neo-functionalist model. This may be particularly true in regard to
neo-functionalist assumptions about the role of national
political elites and interest groups in generating the
"spillovers" which are supposed to move the integration
process along.

Though these concepts will be dealt with thoroughly
in the body of this work, it is necessary to introduce
the neo-functionalist position at this point. Haas made
his clearest statement on the subject in 1970:

> The neo-functional approach rests its claim to fame
> on an extended analogy rather than relying on
> isoporphisms or identities between phenomena. It
> borrows the postulates of actor perception and
> behavoir which are said to explain the character
> of a pluralistically organized national state; it
> notes that certain of these seem to coincide with
> behavior at the regional level and therefore holds
> that the rest of the behavior is also explicable
> in terms of the pluralistic national model. [9]

Extensive exegesis of neo-functionalist studies
sheds some light on what Haas is saying. These thinkers
believe that integration, that is, the creation of a
regional political community, will be spurred most
quickly by the sub-national actors usually defined as
political elites in a pluralist state, for example,
political party activists and trade union and interest
group leaders. These actors are supposed to perceive
over a period of time that the institutions which can
best process their demands are those at the regional
level, and thus gradually shift their political efforts
and their loyalties to that level, developing transnational links in the process.[10] In other words,

political actors will act on the regional level <u>in the</u>
<u>same manner</u> in which they act on the national level.
This is precisely what the French miners were doing
in November 1978 in Strasbourg. The problem is that the
European Parliament could not then and cannot for the
foreseeable future do anything concrete to help with
French employment problems. Replicating group behavior
which succeeds on the national level simply cannot work
in the Community at present.
    It is the concept of "spillover" which addresses
this obvious problem in the neo-functionalist analysis.
According to the theorists, interest groups will gradually perceive that "European" economic decisions are
beyond the range of their influence and will therefore
press for greater political input at the Community
level: "There exists a continuum between economic
integration and political union; the two areas are
linked by an automatic politicization process ('spillover')."[11]
    There is, I think, a possible problem in this
analysis. Groups are supposed to move automatically
toward the European political stage, but what are they
to do when they get there? Will national political
parties, for example, allocate substantial financial
resources for European election campaigns when they know
the Parliament they elect can do little to promote their
constituents' interests at the Community level? Will
these same parties be willing to make the kind of compromises necessary to create transnational groupings
among the parties of the Ten if these groups will be
working to elect a body which is seldom heeded by the
real European decision-making body, the Commission?
    Leon Lindberg once stated what he thinks is the
work of scholars studying regional integration:

> It is the task of students of political integration
> to seek to document the emergence of collective
> decision-making institutions and processes among
> given clusters of nations, to explain how and why
> such efforts are made and how and why they succeed
> or fail, and to build causal theory about the
> nature of political integration as a process and
> its relationship to other aspects of the overall
> integration process.[12]

Having raised several questions about the work of
Lindberg and his colleagues, we will now state what this
study proposes to do in order to carry regional integration research forward.
    This particular research project seeks to focus on
one possible problem in neo-functionalist theorizing:
the relationship of national political groups to the
building of a European political community. The basic
question is whether the European Community institutions

as presently structured provide the impetus for national political elites to react to economic integration by working for political union. In other words, does there exist sufficient motivation to bring about the "spill-overs" which are supposed to lead to political integration? The investigation of group activity at the European level which follows will take the form of a study of the campaign for the first direct elections to the European Parliament. As Karl Kaiser of the German Society for Foreign Affairs noted, direct elections throughout the Community have the potential for changing the substance and focus of European politics and for "creating new trans-national political links in Europe."[13] For example, the major party groupings of the Community, particularly Socialists and Christian Democrats, were working for several years before the 1979 election to form transnational campaign platforms with a European focus.[14]

Close observation of the campaign as waged by several of the major parties involved ought to result in (1) the acquisition of sufficient empirical data to discern whether predictions regarding the integrative potential of the campaign worked out in reality, and (2) some understanding of whether these particular political elites sense it important to commit themselves to transnational politics on a major scale. Having examined those results one ought to be able to return to neo-functionalist theory of how these groups are supposed to function and either add to validation of the theory or pose questions about whether the neo-functionalist method ought to be abandoned by the Community. Haas, as quoted above, believed that pluralist politics would be automatically replicated at the European level. I tend to think that Haas was incorrect because the "political system" of the Community is still too embryonic, that is, there is not sufficient democratically controllable power at the center of the Community to provide political groups with reasons to act on the European level in a manner analogous to their behavior at home.

In order to examine this central tenet of neo-functionalism, the study which follows will investigate several distinct areas and then bring them together. To begin, neo-functionalism and its relationship to the development of an integrated Europe will be analyzed. The major concepts of this body of theory as explicated by its chief spokespersons will be set forth, and it will be shown that, of several schools of regional integration theorizing, it is neo-functionalism which best describes and most influences the "Community method." At the end of the first chapter, then, my particular doubts about the validity of the neo-functionalists' analysis should be clear.

The second chapter will turn to an examination of the three political parties chosen for the case study: the West German Social Democrats (SPD), the Parti Socialiste (PS) of France, and the British Labour Party. The purpose of this chapter is to place these groups in proper historical and ideological context for the study of the European campaign which will follow. An explanation of why these particular parties were chosen for the study seems appropriate. My first concern was to choose parties from a Community political group which had the potential for considerable strength at the European level and which were political forces in most of the nine countries which participated in the first election. These factors are important if transnational linkages are to be investigated and if differing national contexts are to be considered. The choice of groups was quickly narrowed to Christian Democrats and Socialists. In 1979 the Christian Democrats had members in six of the nine countries, the Socialists in all nine.[15] Hence, either group would be valid for a transnational study, but the Socialists - who have historically claimed an internationalist prespective - seemed to have the greatest potential for integrative success, so they were chosen. It seemed unrealistic and unnecessary to follow the campaigns in all nine countries, so Britain, France, and the Federal Republic of Germany were singled out for several reasons: their size and importance in the Community, the major positions occupied by the three parties within the respective countries, and the differing histories of the countries and the particular parties vis-à-vis the Community.

The third and fourth chapters will turn specifically to the direct elections. Chapter three will examine electoral laws, the role of the Confederation of Socialist Parties of the European Community, and the various national and transnational election manifestos. The fourth chapter will discuss the campaign as actually waged by the SPD, PS, and Labour Party, and will conclude with some observations on the degree of integrative activity which took place.

The task of the final chapter is to relate the campaign to the theory. Having discovered what ought to happen according to neo-functionalism and what actually did happen, we should be able to shed some new light on the Community's method of integration, to ascertain whether this dramatic event was able to spur national party groups to act on the European level in the way they act at home. Of course, if this investigation demonstrates that neo-functionalism is not working, the chapter will conclude with some observations on how the European Community might adapt its structures to more effectively promote political integration.

Philippe Schmitter wrote of one of his earlier neo-functionalist analyses that it was a "successful failure" - a failure because he had still not reached the level of theory, a success because in critiquing him others brought integration research closer to real answers.[16] It is in the spirit of what Schmitter calls providing researchers with a new "target" that this project is begun. It will not reach any profound truths, but perhaps it will provide another researcher with the few grains of sand that can evoke a new and better synthesis.

The study of regional integration, as the regional institutions themselves, is by no means neat and decisive. It is, however, almost unique within the kind of political science research which has been done since the mid-fifties. The integrationists struggle to understand something which profoundly matters: a way to organize the world which can insure peace. As Ernst Haas put it: "The main reason for studying regional integration is thus normative: the units and actions studied provide a living laboratory for observing the peaceful creation of possible new types of human communities."[17]

NOTES

1. Personally observed while attending a session of the European Parliament, Palais de l'Europe, Strasbourg, France, Nov. 14, 1978.
2. Lord Wayland Kennet, MEP, and M. Edgar Pisani, MEP, personal interviews, Palais de l'Europe, Strasbourg, France, Nov. 14 and 15, 1978.
3. Karl Kaiser, "Europe's Parliament," New York Times, Feb. 18, 1979, sec. 4, p. 19. Also see Michael Palmer, "The Role of a Directly Elected European Parliament," World Today 33 (April 1977): 122.
4. Charles Pentland, International Theory and European Integration (New York: Free Press, c. 1973), p. 131.
5. Neo-functionalist theory is the subject of Chapter One of the study, and the problem of frequent alterations in the neo-functionalist paradigm is discussed at length therein. It should be noted that the theory has been abandoned by its major architects, but that its principles are embodied in the Treaty of Rome. Thus, while the experts have turned their attention to other matters, the Community still operates according to their prescriptions.
6. Pentland, European Integration, p. 132.
7. Ernst Haas, The Uniting of Europe: Political, Social, and Economic Forces, 1950-1957 (Stanford: Stanford University Press, c. 1968) p. 5.
8. ibid., p. 16.
9. Haas, "The Study of Regional Integration: Reflections on the Joy and Anguish of Pretheorizing,"

International Organization 24 (Winter 1970): 623.
    10. See, for example, the discussion of the role of
elites in Haas, Beyond the Nation State (Stanford, Stanford University Press, c. 1964), pp. 35-40.
    11. Gerhard Mally, The European Community in Per-
spective (Lexington, Mass.: D.C. Heath, Lexington
Books, c. 1973), p. 29.
    12. Leon Lindberg, "Political Integration as a
Multidimensional Phenomenon Requiring Multivariate
Analysis," International Organization 24 (Winter 1970):
650.
    13. Kaiser, "Europe's Parliament."
    14. ibid.
    15. The European Parliament (Luxembourg: Office of
Official Publications of the European Community, 1978),
p. 12.
    16. Philippe Schmitter, "A Revised Theory of
Regional Integration," International Organization 24
(Winter 1970): 836.
    17. Haas, "Regional Integration," p. 608.

1
Neo-Functionalism and the Community Method of Integration

Neo-functionalist writer Philippe Schmitter, reflecting on the experience of doing research in Brussels, commented, "Some of us have had the rather unnerving experience of hearing our special jargon spouted back at us by those whom we are studying." [1] This seemingly casual remark points to the underlying premise of this study: the method of regional integration prescribed by the neo-functionalist school of thought is the method which has been followed by the European Community since the European Coal and Steel Community (ECSC) was expanded by the Treaty of Rome in 1958. It then follows that if the Ten plan political and economic integration according to the tenets of neo-functionalism, any mistaken analyses in this theory will be reflected in the Community's success or failure in bringing about the integration of its member states. Therefore, any study of the integrative potential of a specific activity of the Community, for example, the direct elections to the European Parliament, ought to begin with a thorough examination of neo-functionalism. Only then can the researcher understand exactly how the Community proposes to accomplish its goals and consequently be able to assess its progress.

The purpose of this initial chapter is to undertake this necessary examination of the theoretical underpinnings of the Community. Three objectives must be met in order to accomplish this task: (1) to demonstrate the closely interwoven relationship between European integration and neo-functionalism; (2) to explain the major tenets of neo-functionalist theory; and, (3) to provide a thorough critique of those tenets of the theory which relate to political integration.

Before turning to those concerns it is necessary to take note of the multiplicity of definitions of the relevant terms available to the contemporary political scientist and to indicate those to be used throughout this study. Ernst Haas' definitions of political community and political integration will be adhered to

9

10

whenever those terms are discussed. As cited in the Introduction, according to Haas, political community is
"a condition in which specific groups and individuals
show more loyalty to their central political institutions than to any other political authority," while
political integration is "the process whereby political
actors in several distinct national settings are persuaded to shift their loyalties, expectations and
political activities to a new centre."[2] Haas has several formulations of both definitions, but these, from
The Uniting of Europe, are the clearest and most frequently used.

The concept of federation will appear often in the
pages which follow, and K.C. Wheare's classic definition
will be the meaning intended: federation is "a form of
government in which sovereignty or political power is
divided between the central and local governments, so
that each of them in its own sphere is independent of
the other."[3]

Neo-functionalism, as will be demonstrated later,
has its roots in systems theory and tends to see the
Community as an embryonic Eastonian system. Therefore,
Easton's formulation of the political system as the
authoritative allocator of values and goods in the
society will be employed.[4] Important also is Easton's
concept of the aspects of society which compose this
system:

> These elements of political activity, such as
> governmental organizations, pressure groups,
> voting, parties, and other social elements related
> to them, such as classes, regional groupings, and
> so forth, all show close enough interaction to
> be considered part of the political process.[5]

They will all be considered integral to the Community
system in the pages which follow.

The most difficult definitional task deals with the
Community itself. It is more than an international organization, yet less than a federation. It is also
involved in an evolutionary process toward some vague
concept usually called "Europe." Haas used the term
supranationality to describe it:

> Supranationality in structural terms, therefore,
> means the existence of government authorities clos-
> er to the archtype of federation than any other
> international organization, but not yet identical
> with it. While almost all the criteria point
> positively toward federation, the remaining limits
> on the ability to implement decisions and to expand
> the scope of the system independently still suggest
> the characteristics of international organization.
> However, supranationality in operation - as

distinguished from structure - depends on the
behavior of men and groups of men. It is in this
realm that the final answer to the query may be
found.[6]

This concept, that the Community is unique and still
evolving, seems as relevant today as when formulated in
the late 1950s. Therefore, in the pages to follow the
Community will be treated as a unique supranational
entity, and consequently not compared to any other regional organizations.
Other terms will crop up - neo-functionalism is
replete with them - but with this base our investigation
of the theory can begin.

FUNCTIONALISM ONCE REMOVED

Simplistically stated, it all began with David
Mitrany and a devastating world war. The war and the
need for massive reconstruction provided the impetus
and Mitrany's functionalism provided the method. Thus,
the European Coal and Steel Community (ECSC) was born
in 1953. Stuart Scheingold describes the prevailing
mood in western Europe in the early 1950s:

The precondition in this case was, I believe, that
integration was good by definition since it was
directed at economic reconstruction and permanent
reconciliation between nations whose bloody conflicts had led to major wars engulfing significant
portions of the world. A 'United States of Europe'
seemed almost by definition likely to serve the
cause of a peaceful and prosperous future.[7]

The body of political thought which came to be
called functionalism provided the means for easing
Europe into this kind of unity. Functionalism is rather
simple to grasp if seen as an application of Rousseau's
distinction between the general will and the will of
all. The will of all is "but a sum of private wills,"
that is, interest politics. The general will "regards
only the common interest."[8] To the functionalist the
general will resides in those who are concerned with the
non-political welfare needs of all people: technological
experts. As Pentland describes the distinction,

[T]here is a continuous tension between technological progress and political structure, the former representing man at his rational, adaptive,
and fraternal best, the latter showing him at his
particularistic, destructive, and obscurationist
worst.[9]

There are several elements of this overall description which require explanation because they relate
closely to the idealized model of the ECSC, but not to
the Community. The first is that the functional institutions created to meet specific welfare needs are supposed to gradually wean individual loyalties away from
sovereign nation-states and transfer them to a variety
of institutions. "The dynamics of integration for the
Functionalists is the learning process of citizens who
are gradually drawn into the cooperative ethos created
by the functionally specific international institutions
devoted to the satisfaction of real welfare needs."[10]
Orthodox functionalism presupposes a network of institutions, each performing a specific welfare task.

A second element is that functionalists believe
that the "welfare functions" can be separated from the
political functions, and that the economic welfare
sphere can be taken over by new institutions "without
disturbing the sleeping lion of national sovereignty,
who, upon awakening, realizes that he has become obso-
lete and has been replaced by a new order."[11] The functionalists are not interested in creating a supranational entity; in fact, that strongly oppose such a
project. Mitrany is firmly against the setting up of
"closed political units" by functional means. His
reason? "[If] they are to be closed and exclusive
unions, the more fully and effectively they are integrated the deeper must in fact be the division they cause
in the emergent unity of the world."[12] Functionalism is
not out to create a new center of sovereignty and political power, but rather to diffuse the functions of and
therefore disarm the nation-state. Its adherents argue
that welfare needs are not coterminous with national
boundaries, that a specific welfare need may be coterminous with one set of states, but that a closed regional system does not have the flexibility to meet all
welfare needs of the group's populace.[13]

The European Coal and Steel Community was designed
to be a functionalist institution - administered by
technocrats, independent from the political sphere,
assigned a functionally specific task. In describing
the ECSC Mitrany said, "Such an organ is competent to
manage the activity put in its charge, within the terms
of the agreement, but not to act in any other sectors
of economic and social life of its members, let alone in
any political matter."[14]

Pure functionalism would conclude that the ECSC was
ruined by success. In time its architects confronted
what Schmitter terms the "functionalist paradox." His
analysis is that

The narrower, more separable, and hence more technical, the scope of 'integrated policy-making',
the easier it may be to get initial agreement but

the less significant is likely to be the subsequent impact upon national structures / values and, indirectly, regional processes.[15]

Initial success in one narrow field induced the "Europeans" to broaden their arena and move toward a common market, still modeled closely on ECSC institutions. The expectation was more rapid integration along functionalist lines. As Haas concluded, the decision was along the correct path: "Of all the issues and policy areas the commitment to create a common market is the most conducive to rapid regional integration and the maximization of a spillover."[16]

The creation of the European Economic Community (EEC) disturbed David Mitrany. He was afraid of the incursion of politics into a functionalist institution. He explained that ECSC and Euratom were "straight functional bodies" and that they could therefore "get on with their alloted tasks without offending the position of other countries, while remaining open to link up with them."[17] He feared that the founding of the EEC signaled the end of technical autonomy. As he explained, "Yet it cannot be otherwise: the wider and vaguer the range of its activity, the less is the likelihood that a technical organization would be given the freedom of supranational autonomy."[18]

The purpose here is not to evaluate functionalism, but the question of how the functionalist ECSC was actually transformed by the founding of the EEC is a provocative one. Particularly pertinent to this study is the notion of technical self-determination. Was the ECSC really responsible to the general will and not the will of all? Pentland concluded that the Coal and Steel Community was never immune to politics. "Pressure groups, parties, and change of regime mattered greatly."[19] Ernst Haas, in Beyond the Nation State, addresses this aspect of the functionalist analysis and finds the notion of pure technocracy to be a false description of the real world:

We banish from our construct the notion that individual actors, groups, or elites regularly and predictably engage in political pursuits for unselfish reasons. All political action is purposively linked with individual or group perception of interest. While the unseen hand may somehow hold a system of opposing perceptions and clashing interests together, we reject the notion of any natural harmony of interests based on purposive, calculated behavior. We further reject the notion of conscience, good will, dedication to the common good, or subservience to a socially manipulated consensus on welfare questions, as possessing little consistent reality in living politics. Co-

operation among groups is thus the result of con-
vergences of separate perceptions of interest and
not a spontaneous surrender to the myth of the
common good.[20]

This understanding on the part of a writer who began his
scholarly career in sympathy with the functionalist notion of integration aids us in grasping one element of
the European experiment: it has always been economics
harnessed to serve political interests, not separated
from them. In this sense, as will be more fully explored later in this chapter, neo-functionalism, with
its emphasis on interest group theory, better explains
the European reality.

The Haas definition of political integration also
points to the conclusion that neo-functionalism best
describes what is happening among the Ten. He is concerned with a shift in individual loyalties "toward a
new centre", not toward a variety of functional institutions.[21] Traveling in the Community recently, I encountered a group of unemployed young people on their
way to demonstrate in Brussels. Why Brussels? "Because
it has become the capital of Europe."[22] It is perhaps
unscholarly to base a conclusion on the remark of an
unnamed young man of undertermined nationality and background, but his unscientific response tells much about
what Europeans see happening.

Not only is the establishment of one regional center of power a neo-functionalist concept, the goal of
the process is distinctly neo-functionalist. Gerald
Mally wrote in 1973, "In short, the European Community
is a pluralistic system in evolution from nationalism
to regionalism using economic integration as a means of
promoting political unity."[23] Another student of the
recent European experience views the Community as an
attempt to use functionalist means to reach federalist
goals. About the method he says, "It is neo-functionalist in that it does not change or eliminate the essence of politics but only moves through functional
methods to a higher (federal) level what traditional
functionalism wants to eliminate in the first place."[24]

To the extent that the European Community is subject to pressures from interest groups and political
parties and thus lacks functional autonomy, it is best
described by neo-functionalist writers. Furthermore,
to the extent that the Ten seek eventual political
unity, they are following a neo-functionalist approach.
On the other hand, neo-functionalism's ambiguous statements about the roles of politicians vs. "experts",
the reluctance to postulate a specific end point toward
which the EEC should be working, and the failure of
integration to come as smoothly and easily as predicted
also point out in a negative sense the reliance of the
Community on neo-functionalism. These questions, and

the difficult problem of pinning down <u>exactly</u> what
neo-functionalism is, must now be considered.

THE NEO-FUNCTIONALIST THEORY OF INTEGRATION

Neo-functionalism is the label given to a substantial body of political thought about regional integration which has been developed since the late 1950s.
Its name provides the link with its origin: neo-functionalists rely on the method of pure functionalism but
apply it to a new arena: the regional political system.
This body of political writing is not a theory in the
formal sense of the term, but rather a group of hypotheses about how a regional system can come to be integrated. Its chief proponents have been American political scientists, most notably Ernst Haas and his
student Leon Lindberg. Neo-functionalism has three
intellectual precursors - functionalism, systems theory,
and pluralist interest group theory - and weaves them
together to create a still evolving explanation of the
dynamics of regionalization.

This "theory" does not lend itself to easy and
systematic analysis for several reasons. The first is
the most difficult: it constantly shifts its emphasis
over time, most often in <u>reaction</u> to events in the
European Community or other regional groupings. Second,
its hypotheses have been developed by a group of political scientists who do not always agree with each
other. Third, each individual writer has developed his
own terminology and set of definitions, in addition to
which several of these researchers change <u>their</u> <u>own</u>
terminology with each new article they pro<u>duce. The</u>
neo-functionalists have been quite successful at being
"moving targets" and hence quite difficult to discuss.
Nevertheless, their relationship with the Community
makes the task of pinning them down an imperative one.

The neo-functionalist shift from pure functionalism
to an analysis of interest groups has been discussed
above. Five other aspects of the theory must be examined here: (1) its reliance on systems and pluralist
theories; (2) the question of dependent variables; (3)
the role of elites, groups, and political actors; (4)
the concept of spillover; and (5) the problem of regional institution building. These major concepts will be
discussed in turn, and in each case the writings of
several of the representative thinkers will be employed.
In exploring each aspect of the theory the approach will
be a search for commonalities which can lead to general-
izations. This method should provide the insights
necessary to sketch a broad picture of what neo-functionalism in fact says about integration.

Systems Theory and Pluralist Democracies

Leon Lindberg is the neo-functionalist who most clearly pays his intellectual debts to David Easton. In 1970 Lindberg wrote, "Systems analysts like David Easton focus directly on what I have chosen to accept as the distinctly political, that is, the system of interactions through which binding or authoritative allocations are made and implemented."[25] In an earlier article Lindberg employed the Almond and Coleman categories of functions in a political system and found five relevant to the European Community: political socialization, interest articulation, interest aggregation, political communication, and decision output. He then suggested the use of these categories in empirical studies of the "evolution of transactions at every level between the politics of the Community and those of the member states."[26] He thus makes it quite clear that his notions of how to analyze a political system are based on the works of American structural-functionalists and systems theorists.

Other neo-functionalists do not tend to be as explicit as Lindberg in discussing the origins of their concepts, but the parameters within which they work, their attention to the roles of non-governmental actors, their lack of emphasis on formal political institutions, their employment of such terms as "system overload", "communications function", and "feedback" make the source of their ideas quite clear.[27] They stem from the mainstream of American political science as it was studied in the 1950s and 1960s.

Another group of recent American political analysts focuses on pluralism and the "end of ideology." These writers have a remote connection with Mitrany and his de-emphasis of the distinctly political. Threads of pluralist thought turn up repeatedly in neo-functionalist analysis. Paul Taylor discusses this point and finds one neo-functionalist in particular who is a pluralist: "Professor Haas rejects Gemeinschaft and substitutes for it a pluralist model of society, a kind of community of competing interests which co-exist because of an agreement about the rules of the game within a constitutional system."[28] Taylor's point is well taken. Haas, in Beyond the Nation State, says that the modern state "looks and acts much like the Gesellschaft we associate with our international system. Instead of being intimate and cozy, it functions like a large-scale bureaucratic organization." He goes on to point out that the nation-state today does not perform for its citizens the function of "aggregating all their demands and hopes into a general consensus."[29] The point Haas is making is that the pluralist model is easily applicable to an international system in the same way that it works in an individual state.[30]

Haas' clearest formulations about postindustrial, nonideological politics are found in "Technocracy, Pluralism, and the New Europe," written in 1963. Here he asserts:

Indeed, when we turn to the political style of the New Europe, perhaps indifference is the key term. Political parties remain intact; but they are no longer divided by glaring controversy because all the major social and economic issues of fifty years ago no longer plague the body politic.[31]

Lindberg does not go as far as Haas in his statements on this issue, but he strikes a similar chord: "Politics has not been emptied of its emotional, symbolic, or dramatic content, yet that content is no longer dominant for most actors."[32] These ideas about postindustrial politics are partly developed from neo-functionalist observation of the Community system which still emphasizes the role of the experts on the Commission rather than the traditional roles of elected political leaders. At the same time - and this is the constant dynamic between neo-functionalism and the Community - one senses that the "Eurocrats" rely on the neo-functionalists to bolster their position of technical supremacy.

Systems theorists, structural-functionalists, and pluralists have all contributed to the development of neo-functionalism. They provided the seeds for a new analysis of international politics. However, the greater part of neo-functionalist thought moves beyond its antecedents and into the problem of discovering which actors and what types of forces can transform a regional system into a new pluralist political community. We now turn to neo-functionalism proper.

The Elusive Dependent Variable

One of the greatest difficulties posed for those who seek to understand the neo-functionalists is the question of where they are going. Though they have been accused of being teleogical in their arguments they have steadfastly refused to posit one clear end point toward which they expect a regional system to move. A glance at some of their statements on the subject makes the point quite adequately. Haas says,

The verbally defined single terminal conditions with which we worked in the past - political community, security community, political union, federal union - are inadequate because they foreclose real-life possibilities.[33]

Writing in the same issue of the same journal, Philippe
Schmitter posits two dimensions of the dependent variable: "Whether member states will expand or contract the
type of issues to be resolved jointly (scope) or whether
they will increase or decrease the authority for regional institutions to allocate values (level)."[34]
    Citing each other's formulations on the subject is
a favorite undertaking. J.S. Nye singles out one of
Haas' paradigms, this one developed with Schmitter, and
notes that their dependent variable "automatic politicization" (which is closely akin to another central
concept - "spillover") is an ambiguous term.[35] Haas,
meanwhile, investigates the possible outcomes in the
Lindberg - Scheingold construct and finds three: fulfillment, retraction, or extension of tasks assigned to
the regional organization.[36]
    J.S. Nye comes closest to clarity in naming and
explaining a dependent variable:

    Our choice of collective decisionmaking in the
    policies involved in an economic union has the
    virtue of closeness to the manifest motives and
    interests of the actors involved in integration
    schemes in less developed states, as well as close-
    ness to what seems to be the 'neither fish nor
    fowl' institutional shape of the current integra-
    tion process in Europe.[37]

    The few previous paragraphs beg for some analysis.
Because these scholars do not clearly label the condition which would be the achievement of the neo-functionalist goal, that is, the dependent variable, it is
very difficult for them to be specific about the variables whose increase would point to the approach of this
goal. In other words, they discuss the means to an end
without explicitly defining that end. The Lindberg -
Scheingold outcomes, for example, are fancy words for
standing still, backsliding, or moving forward. They
indeed exhaust the possibilities of any dynamic situation and at the same time provide no useful insights.
The end point postulated by Haas in 1958 - "political
community" - is a concept devoid of institutional description, but by 1970 he would not even accept this
loose construct as an ultimate goal. Even Nye's choice,
collective decisionmaking, lacks explanatory value because he does not seem concerned about who makes the
collective decisions. Is there a difference among
decisions made by unanimous consent of the Council of
Ministers, majority vote of a Commission of technical
experts, or through deliberations of a directly elected
and sovereign legislature? There is, I think, a tre-
mendous difference which the neo-functionalists tend to
ignore.
    There is another aspect of the discussion of the

dependent variable. This is the body of criticism which tries to prove that the neo-functionalists know quite well what they would like to see in Europe, but refuse to say so for "political" reasons. This problem, the teleological nature of neo-functionalist theorizing, will be taken up later in this chapter. For the moment it is enough to say that the neo-functionalists are consistently elusive about the institutional outcomes they expect from political and economic integration.

Elites, Groups, and Political Actors

Neo-functionalists are concerned with transferring political loyalties of individuals to a new regional center. They reject the functionalist tendency to ignore the presence of interest groups in societies, and in fact place great emphasis on the role of political and economic elites and pluralist groups in bringing about further integration. Therefore, they write a great deal about the function of groups and elites in the process of regional transformation. It should also be noted as we take up this facet of their thought that the role of political actors in the neo-functionalist scheme is germane to this study. One last introductory comment: the neo-functionalist analysis of individual actors is confined to the elite level. Little mention is ever made of mass perceptions regarding integration.
Groups and elites are approached by these writers from several different directions: the necessity of elite support for the integration process, the way in which the Community's existence affects elites, the function of elite socialization, and the formation of transnational groupings. Each of these aspects deserves some attention because elites are viewed as the glue which holds the integration project together.
Charles Pentland summarizes the importance of elite support in the neo-functionalist framework. He concludes that the success of the regional system largely depends on "the type and level of demands made on it, the "systematic support' offered it by elites and publics, and the leadership resources available to it on the national and supranational levels."[38] The theorists themselves offer numerous explanations of why elites are important. Haas says that the integration process cannot get off the ground without some actor perception of interdependence. "Their initial commitment includes a shared conception of how and why they need one another."[39] Nye adds:

Functionally specific, universalistic, achievement-oriented groups in all member states were important components of the neo-functionalist path in Europe. Our hypothesis is that the greater the pluralism

in all member states, the better the conditions for
an integrative response to the feedback from the
process forces.[46]

Political actors are important to Haas and his
colleagues, and not necessarily because these actors are
cognizant of and sympathetic with long range integration
goals. As Haas himself notes, "Moreover, neo-functionalists rely on the primacy of incremental decisionmaking
over grand designs, arguing that most political actors
are incapable of long-range purposive behavior."[41]
Lindberg and Scheingold give a slightly different emphasis to the same issue. They believe that interest
groups in Europe have come to see the Community as a
fait accompli and act accordingly:

> They may or may not be convinced 'integrationists.'
> They may or may not favor extending the scope of
> joint decision-making. The point is that the ex-
> istence of the Community alters their situation,
> and they must adjust their goals and political ac-
> tivities accordingly.[42]

Actor perception that Brussels and Strasbourg are appropriate places in which to lobby for any concrete political or economic goal is the issue of importance here. It
matters to none of these scholars whether interest group
leadership is concerned about "building Europe". The
crucial point is that these leaders strengthen the
legitimacy and consequently the powers of the Community
every time they try to use their infulence to affect the
decisions of any European Community organ.
    Elite socialization becomes highly relevant in this
context. National civil servants, parties, and pressure
groups are supposed to gradually perceive the ways in
which the Europe of the Ten can assist them. This is
particularly important because the Community and its
own already established European elite can easily be
viewed as unwelcome competition to national leadership.
J.S. Nye, Lindberg, and Stuart Scheingold all touch upon
this theme. Nye sees the solution to the dilemma in
choosing "process mechanisms" which have the potential
capability of bringing national political and economic
leadership into close touch with their European counterparts.[43]   Lindberg and Scheingold believe the problem
can be solved in terms of practical payoffs:

> The other set of elites has policy preoccupations,
> needs, and ambitions which may impel them to view
> the European system solely in terms of its contri-
> bution to other goals which transcend the economic
> or welfare spheres, or the political effort to
> unify a long-divided Europe.[44]

Elite perception of the promise the European arena holds for them can ease the task of the Eurocrats. It has, according to neo-functionalists, an even more potent outcome: it causes national interest groups to organize regionally, thus strengthening the skeletal transnational system. Regional group integration is, according to these theorists, both a source of still further integration and a result of an initially successful regional system. As will be seen shortly, there is ample surface evidence to substantiate their claims that this regional group process is happening in Europe, but much other evidence that these regional interest groups are merely coordinators while real decisional power remains at the national level.

Philippe Schmitter's formulation on emerging regional groups provides a good introduction:

> These 'subnational actors', each with their respective strategies, combine into stable 'transnational coalitions' of support and opposition. The policy vector now becomes the product of alliances which cut across national boundaries (and, perhaps, historic national cleavages).[45]

Other neo-functionalist writers tend toward the same line of hypothesizing. Nye discusses the formation of "formal and informal nongovernmental regional organizations" which will supposedly aid in shifting political activity to the regional level, pressure national governments toward further integration, and continue the process of elite socialization.[46] Lindberg comments on the importance of regional interest groups in the Common Agricultural Policy (CAP) negotiations, and finds that "groups and elites in all countries" believed they had a stake in those negotiations.[47]

Ernst Haas, as Paul Taylor notes, "puts primary stress upon changes in behaviour among institutional elites."[48] Haas, most often in his earlier works, frequently took up the subject of regional group formation. An example of his thinking:

> The character of decision-making stimulates interest groups to make themselves heard; it spurs political parties in Strasbourg and Luxembourg to work out common positions; it creates an enormous pressure on high national civil servants to get to know and establish rapport with their opposite numbers.[49]

This attention, given on the one hand to the automatic tendency of interest groups to align transnationally and on the other to the beneficent effects of such coalition building, is at the core of the neo-functionalist argument.

However, little work has been done in actually assessing the degree of integration among interest groups
and even less has been aimed at transnational cooperation among political parties. What has been accomplished is the drawing up of several sets of hypotheses
about these groups. Schmitter's, which is representative, identifies several variables which are presumed
to affect integration among interest groups. Among
them are: increasing and varied transnational transactions, increase in internal pluralism in member
states, acquisition of similar expectations among com-
plementary elites, the degree of autonomy of regional
interest groups, the degree of development of a regional
identity, and the degree of perceived effect of individual participation.[50] These categories are of interest
in that they isolate several of the tasks which must be
accomplished as national groups integrate with their
European peers, but they provide precious little in the
way of clues to aid persons trying to design a successful integration scheme. In fact, a major question which
arises as one studies neo-functionalist hypotheses about
integration among groups is why they expect these groups
to come together in the first place. While these theorists develop elaborate typologies to identify categories of interaction which foster integration, they ignore the question of how the Community decision-making
process motivates groups to act in concert with their
peers from among the Ten.

Groups and elites, because they are the actors
presumed to operationalize the two facets of neo-functionalist theory yet to be discussed - spillover and
institutionalization - will figure often in the remainder of this chapter. Nevertheless, the major themes of
this discussion about them should be pulled together at
this time for the sake of clarity. First, we recall
that pluralist groups and the elites who lead them are
absolutely pivotal to the integration process because
their perception of gains to be realized through transnational activity is the dynamic which sets the process
in motion. Therefore, elite socialization in the form
of any regional interaction should have positive results. The most important results are the formation of
transnational groups who look to the Community institutions as the authoritative allocators of values and
goods, and therefore legitimate these institutions.

We turn now to examine the process in which groups
participate at the regional level and the outcomes which
are expected if the process is successful, according to
the neo-functionalists.

Spillover

The analysis of any body of theoretical material
unfortunately requires its component parts to be tem-

porarily isolated. Thus, their innate relationship is
sometimes obscured in the process of piece-by-piece examination. A word is in order then about the relationship between pluralist groups and the abstract concept
of "spillover". Interest groups and the elites who
compose them are seen to be central forces in the integration process, as has been discussed. The mechanism they are supposed to generate is "spillover" or
"automatic politicization". As they are the key actors,
spillover is the key process on the road to a new political community. This phenomenon of growing politicization will be examined here in terms of its definition,
its importance, and how it is expected to work. Lastly,
some of the changes in neo-functionalist hypothesizing
on this concept will be discussed.

This dynamic, which may be briefly described as a
ripple effect generated by interaction at the regional
level among national elites, is at the core of the
neo-functionalist logic. Of all neo-functionalist
terms, spillover seems to be the most ambiguous. One of
the clearest explanations of this concept was written by
Haas and Schmitter:

> ...integration can be conceived as involving the
> gradual politicization of actors' purposes which
> were initially considered 'technical' or 'non-
> controversial'. Politicization implies that the
> actors, in response to miscalculation or disap-
> pointment with respect to the initial purposes,
> agree to widen the spectrum of means considered
> appropriate to attain them. This tends to in-
> crease the controversial component, i.e., those
> additional fields of action which require political
> choices concerning how much national autonomy to
> delegate to them. Politicization implies that
> actors seek to resolve their problems so as to
> upgrade common interests and, in the process,
> delegate more authority to the center.[51]

The basic component of this construct, that new problems
will require new powers which will be granted to the new
center, is also the basis of Lindberg's and Nye's explanations of spillover. Lindberg refers to new situations "that can be dealt with only by further expanding
the task and the grant of power,"[52] while Nye reasons
that "If, over the course of time. positive responses to
the process forces lead to higher levels of integration
(stronger institution and greater coordination of economic policy) we would expect the process to become more
'political'."[53]

All of the works cited above were written before
the Community's crisis in the early 1970s, at a time
when integration was proceeding more quickly than anticipated, and when it was thought that economic coop-

eration would flow naturally into political integration.
There was still no anticipation of what later came to be
called "spillback". During that same early period Haas
wrote that spillover was the "essence of supranationality" and was confident that it would "arise from and
further influence the political aspirations of the major
groupings and parties."[54] Though the confidence of
these theorists was somewhat abated by the political
realities of the 1970s, it is important to recall that
until the first direct elections of June 1979 the Community was still structured according to theories which
expected spillover from economic to political realms to
be automatic, as it still is today.

The actual dynamic of spillover as originally con-
ceived revolves around interest groups who demand input
into the integration process controlled by technocrats.
Nye explains this in terms of "new forces of sector
imbalance or engrenage" which will increasingly involve
an escalating number of social groups focusing their
activity at the regional level.[55] This concept is further refined by Nye himself and several of his colleagues. Haas adds an interesting insight, pointing
out that spillover can even be generated by actors who
are not at all concerned with the region's integrative
goals. His analysis is that elites guided by no more
than narrow self-interest may well perceive that this
interest will be best served by politicizing decision-
making at the regional center.[56] Primary attention to
the role of groups also figures in Schmitter's works.
He believes that "spillover is increasingly likely to
occur as the result of package deals designed to appeal
to a broad transnational coalition of interests."[57] Nye
even has a name for transnational coalition formation:
"cultivated spillover". Its difference from "pure
spillover" is that instead of cross-national groups
sharing a common perception of problems and solutions
these groups put together a package deal which provides
a "balance of benefits" to the various national groupings.[58] Cultivated spillover is not automatic; it is
politically contrived integration.

At the outset of this examination of neo-functionalism it was mentioned that the theory goes through
many changes over time and that these changes seem to be
a reaction to developments in the real world of the Community. This is particularly true in regard to the concept of spillover, which was viewed as automatic and inevitable in its earliest formulations. In 1970 J.S. Nye
wrote that the original formulation was "oversimplified
and therefore misleading."[59] At the same time Haas commented that a "proliferation of organizational channels
in a region" may be a stimulus to greater interdependence, but positive results cannot be automatically
predicted.[60]

Pentland's analysis of shifts in the spill-

over concept is that conceptual refinement began almost
as soon as The Uniting of Europe was written. He points
out that in this work Haas "came close to asserting the
inevitability of spillover," but since that time neo-
functionalists have generally retreated from any universal and deterministic claims for this process.[61] As the
neo-functionalists refined/shifted their position they
were seeing two problems in the original construct. The
first was the contention that economic integration would
flow into the political sphere. Haas himself reached
the "inevitable conclusion that functional contexts are
autonomous."[62] The second problem was treated in our
discussion of elites: national elites can and will block
spillover if they perceive that their interests are
threatened by further integration.

In concluding this discussion of spillover, several
major themes deserve repetition. The first is that politicization was first thought to be an automatic outcome of economic integration, and therefore the Community was structured with the expectation that economic integration would flow into political integration. Secondly, the neo-functionalists backed down from this
first formulation, presumably because they saw that it
was inaccurate. However, the structures established by
the Treaty of Rome remained essentially unchanged.

In other words, although the neo-functionalists are
no longer defending the validity of their original formulation about the process of spillover, the European
Community's leadership has continued to expect the neo-
functionalist method of integration to bring about political unification.

In the midst of little institutional change over
the years, the first potentially significant departure
from the technocratic method of Community decision-
making was the first direct election. Even as the Ten
prepare for the second election in 1984, whether these
periodic exercises in democracy will generate further
political integration remains to be seen. It is perhaps
the critical test of neo-functionalism's core concept.

Institution Building

The neo-functionalists' position on the growth of
regional political institutions follows logically from
their analysis of the role of groups in bringing about
integration. Stated briefly, institutions are an important outcome of the regional process, that is, they
are a measure of the success of the integration project.
It is on this point that neo-functionalists stand in the
clearest contrast to federalists. Though both seem to
posit the same end point, for the federalists institutions are the cause, while for the neo-functionalists
they are the effect.

Paul Taylor, who attempts to prove how similar

neo-functionalism and federalism are, develops a view on
the centrality of institutional growth in the neo-functionalist construct which is narrower than most of their
own anaylses. Taylor states:

Institutional spill-over and the learning process
of bureaucrats is substituted for the older Functionalists' integrative dynamic of the learning
experience of citizens. And, as they concentrate
on institutional developments and not upon the
emergence of socio-psychological community, they
implicitly accept the view that sovereignty is$_{63}$
strengthened by an expanding legal competence.

Though Taylor is correct in concluding that institutional growth is important to neo-functionalists, it seems
that his emphasis is misplaced in that Haas and his
colleagues by no means dismiss the growth of "socio-
psychological community". Rather, they expect this
event to spill over into a strengthening of central institutions. This becomes apparent as one examines
their own writings.
     Lindberg and Scheingold, writing in 1966, stated
that the growth of the Community depends upon "its
success in broadening its constituency, upon how well
that constituency is served."[64] Their measure of how
successfully this is being done is the decision-making
capacity of Community institutions. In another later
article Lindberg points out that this decision-making
capacity can only be increased by national elites who
become used to ongoing cooperation on the regional
level and gradually give up "some of the factual attrib-
utes of national sovereignty."[65] Ernst Haas' interpretation of the development of the integration process is
similar. Scheingold concludes that to Haas "the growth
of a pluralist political arena in the context of effective community institutions indicates successful integration."[66] Haas himself pointed out in The Uniting of
Europe that "economic integration unaccompanied by the
growth of central institutions and policies does not
necessarily lead to political community."[67]
     As has been demonstrated, for the neo-functional-
ists institutional growth is pivotal to the success of
regional integration. What is interesting and troubling
about this analysis is that the neo-functionalists do
not ever explain in concrete terms how these institutions are supposed to emerge. They give a few clues,
but no developmental plan. Nye thinks that rising
transactions can lead to "the intensification of central
institutional capacity to handle a particular task," but
is concerned that institutional scope may not be broad-
ened.[68] He develops a concept called "authority -
legitimacy transfer" and would measure institutional
growth according to two indices: authority transferred

to the regional from the national level, and the legitimacy of that authority in the eyes of political actors.[69] These are interesting indicators for designing empirical tests, but they provide no guidelines about how the desired outcomes can be brought about.

The attribute of the process of institutionalization which seems most clear is that it is gradual, or "incremental" as Lindberg expresses it.[70] Other than that, we know that institutional growth is viewed as a sign of successful integration, that it is a result of the spillover process, and that it is set in motion by elites. Questions as to the type of institutions, how quickly they should develop, the place of democratic control in this scheme, and how institutions can actually be formed, are left unanswered.

The intellectual heritage and major tenets of neofunctionalism have now been examined. Our next task is to take what we know about neo-functionalist theory and subject it to a critique. Having done this, we will be able to place the theory in perspective in order to use it as the basis for an examination of the direct elections to the European Parliament.

CRITICAL OBSERVATIONS ON NEO-FUNCTIONALIST THEORY

In the previous pages neo-functionalism and its relationship with the European Community were discussed. With this foundation, it is possible to investigate the problematic aspects of the theory. The problems, of which there are several, tend to fall into two categories which I shall call theoretical and ideological. Several of the criticisms to be offered here concentrate on the intellectual shortcomings of the neo-functionalist argument, while others point to difficulties with the political preconceptions on which the theory is based.

My theoretical critique will discuss the teleological nature of the theory, the problem of engendering spillover, and the question of central institution building. Ideologically, two themes will be addressed: the heavy weight given to pluralism and the "end of ideology", and neo-functionalism's anti-democratic tendencies.

Theoretical Critique

It was stressed earlier in this chapter that neofunctionalists never state an explicit end point toward which they propose the regional system evolves. Though Haas and others refer to such vague concepts as "political community" they never define in institutional terms

exactly what they are driving at. There are two possible explanations for their position: either they hon-
estly do not know or care where European integration is
going, or that they do in fact know what they want and
care very much about its evolution. This point is not
an aside or an attack for the sake of argument. Rather,
I hope to demonstrate that neo-functionalism's method
for achieving political integration is faulty, a criticism that would have little validity if its proponents
did not have a goal.

Neo-functionalist theory is strongly teleological,
that is, it argues for steps toward one specific end
point which its theorists will not admit. I think that
end point is a federal state in Europe, and that, for
political reasons the theorists will not admit this
goal. As Paul Taylor notes,

> The Neo-functionalists seem to fall squarely into
> that American tradition which sees Federalism as
> providing a political solution; it is not necessary
> to the stability of the political system that it
> should be co-extensive with a socio-psychological
> community.[71]

Another critic of integration theory, Charles
Pentland, spends some time discussing the teleological
implications of neo-functionalism. After discussing this
issue Pentland concludes:

> In the early optimistic years of the European Com-
> munity it was generally assumed that the terminal
> point of the integrative process would be some sort
> of federal state in western Europe. Those involved
> in the Community often described themselves as
> working toward a European federation by functional
> means. This self-image, combined with the early
> successes of the Community, tended to reinforce
> neofunctionalist practice and theory alike in its
> assumption about continuous growth toward supra-
> national federation.[72]

Pentland singles out Leon Lindberg as the theorist
who best escapes teleological implications,[73] but in
reading Lindberg one finds that he slips into the pattern of his colleagues: "The essence of political integration is the emergence or creation over time of collec-
tice decisionmaking processes, i.e., political institutions to which governments delegate decisionmaking
authority."[74] Lindberg does not define these institutions as those of a central government in a federal
system - no neo-functionalist is that blunt - but it is
difficult to understand what else he means by delegating
decisional power to new institutions.
    Ernst Haas is quite elusive in his discussions

of the end point of the integrative process, but once
again what he is implying gradually becomes clear. In
his earlier writings, as previously discussed, Haas
called for a "political community" of institutionally
undefined character. He then moved into a period of
postulating three possible outcomes: a "regional state,"
a "regional commune," or an "assymmetrical overlapping."
A regional commune "assumes the kind of interdependence
among the participating units which does not permit the
identification of a single center of authority," and an
assymmetrical overlapping is much like the old functionalist model of a patchwork of international bodies.[75]
He proceeds to describe the regional state as the one
form which will evoke a "regional nationalism" as its
basis for legitimacy.[76] What is regional nationalism if
not a "new political community?"

In the mid-seventies, perhaps because of the stagnation within the Community itself, Haas became less
optimistic about the future of Europe, but he did not
retreat from his unstated goal. In a 1976 evaluation of
European integration he wrote:

> Disjointed incrementalism, then, was the preferred
> strategy of European decisionmakers as long as the
> shared objective was the attainment of a plural-
> istic security community by gradual steps, fanning
> out from an initial dramatic commitment to a common
> market, which was to lead to political union, how-
> ever defined institutionally. The objective was
> constant, the tactic and means variable.[77]

What Haas was trying to do in this particular article was to explain why integration had slowed down in
Europe during the 1970s. However, his evaluation of the
goals of the process and the institutional outcomes
still seems to be based on the notion of a federal
state. In fact, in an earlier passage he argues that
the lack of constant progress toward federation should
not be viewed as a failure, but that what was thought to
be "an intermediate situation - labeled 'confederation'
or 'concordance' - may well become permanent."[78]

What Haas and Lindberg do throughout their writings
is to deny on the one hand that they have a clear goal
in sight, and on the other evaluate the success of the
Community in terms of only one goal: federation. Haas
tries to get out of this dilemma with a device he calls
"action paths." To employ this method, one lists independent variables which can "describe the attainment
of any one of the postulated outcomes," and then scores
a regional organization according to how far it has
traveled on one or all of the paths.[79] This ia an interesting concept, but it is not seriously employed.
One cannot find work by any neo-functionalist rating the
European Community on its success at becoming an "assym-

metrical overlapping." What becomes obvious is that,
although Haas and his colleagues postulate a range of
possible outcomes, the only one they seriously study is
the degree of progress toward central decision-making
within a regional group.
Quite simply, when neo-functionalist theorists
attempt to ascertain the success of the Community,
they rate it on its attainment of centralized, collective decision-making. They ignore the institutional
content, a point which will be discussed shortly, but as
Pentland rightly observes,

> [T]he model of the emergent federation still pro-
> vides most of the standards by which the success or
> failure of integration is measured; the use of
> scales of centralization of decision-making sug-
> gests that this model remains a working assumption
> of many neo-functionalists.[80]

In summarizing this phase of my argument, I think
it important to note that there is nothing wrong per se
with establishing eventual federation as the goal of
European integration. The problem with neo-functionalist theory is more complex. These writers seem to have
made a normative decision that federation is the goal of
the integration process, albeit a normative decision
they will not flatly admit. If federation is the goal,
the "Community method" for which they are largely responsible ought to be the best possible means of reaching it. The contention of this study is that it is not.
The concept of spillover and the role of elites in
bringing about this process have already been discussed.
While this study does not intend to play down the importance of national bureaucrats, political parties, labor
unions, and interest groups in general in the integration process, it is vital to evaluate the validity of
the spillover hypothesis. A major question is whether
spillover is happening, or if the neo-functionalists
have overstated their case about this phenomenon.
Lindberg describes the atmosphere in which further
integration can flourish:

> The theory of integration and of the spillover
> process ... assumes the existence of a pluralistic
> political system governed by the traditions and
> assumptions of democracy and constitutionalism in
> which governing elites are obliged to take into
> account the values, interests, and preoccupations
> of the major organized interests.[81]

It is obvious that the type of system Lindberg describes
is operative within each of the Community's member
states. It is less obvious, but equally true, that the
European Community today has only embryonic traces of

such a political system. Therefore, one must ask quite seriously whether major European interests are organizing at the Community level because of a need to impact governing elites at that level. Brussels is replete with European offices representing interest groups of all sorts. J.S. Nye discusses these confederations:

In general, however, these regional nongovernmental organizations remain a weak force. In many cases the types of interests that are aggregated at the regional level tend to be very general, with more specific interests and structures remaining at the national level. For instance, despite the existence of regional trade union secretariats in Brussels, the idea of collective bargaining at the European level has not taken hold.[82]

Nye makes clear one important differentiation: one can count the number of regional confederations operative in Europe and attain one view of the success of elite integration, or one can look into what these groups are really about and come to an opposite conclusion. If one sees little of substance happening, it is worthwhile to investigate further. In discussing the micro-level attitude change which should be the spill-over catalyst, Pentland concludes, "this is the level of analysis on which neo-functionalism seems to have made the least progress."[83] Mally looks at the problem from a different perspective, but draws a similar conclusion: "However, there appears to be a consensus that while economic integration has been fairly successful, political unification has not progressed at the same pace over the last two decades."[84] It is possible that the weakness of neo-functionalists' analysis on this issue is caused by the way they view regional groups. Such questions as why and by whom a European confederation was founded, who finances it, and what are the advantages and disadvantages of membership might well be posed in order to shed further light on elite integration. In a later chapter, this study will address these questions in discussing the Community's Confederation of Socialist Parties.

Several points can now be gathered together: Lindberg argues that integration fares best within a pluralistic system which must respond to groups. Nye finds European groups to be more show than substance. Pentland and Mally both find political integration among elites to be less than successful. Perhaps Lindberg is correct in his assessment of necessary preconditions, though incorrect in his early assumption that such preconditions existed in the Community.[85] All of this leads to an observation that something is wrong in the spillover dynamic. There are several possibilities, but

the scanty evidence thus far shown tends toward an educated guess that the problem lies in the area of motivation. Why have a regional labor union if contracts are
negotiated at the national level? Why a regional political party if the type of tough compromising this would
require can have no impact on political decisions which
affect voters? Neo-functionalists anticipate a replica-
tion of national level political activity on the regional level before the transnational organization has an
institutional structure comparable to the western nation-state. They believe that the notion of being European must precede the institutional creation of Europe.
The Community institutions are quite another story.
Their development, supposed to be generated by spillover, has stagnated according to some observers. Lindberg notes,

> One of the peculiarities of the Community system is
> the fact that so many of its present structural
> features were intended to be only instrumental and
> temporary. Their infusion with value and their
> development into a quasi-permanent set of institu-
> tions would thus constitute an unanticipated con-
> sequence.[86]

Notwithstanding the fact that the direct elections have
affected some minor changes in the European Parliament,
and the fact that some extra-institutional growth has
occurred,[87] the institutions have remained essentially
unchanged and unchallenged since the Treaty of Rome was
signed. If they were meant to develop further, as Lindberg indicates, the mechanism to bring about this development was left to the design of political actors - and
they have not acted.
   The lack of institutional growth can, of course,
be brought back to a critique of the spillover hypothesis, and a circular argument can proceed indefinitely.
However, one aspect of the link still deserves mention.
Spillover is set into motion by a disequilibrium in the
system. If political elites do not receive massive
pressure for or against integration, they do not act. As
Nye observes:

> If mass opinion is not intense in one direction or
> the other, the 'normal' reaction of decisionmakers
> is not to decide ....the result would be the middle
> course of the status quo. In short, our hypothe-
> sized expectation is inertia.[88]

A cursory glance at any of the Eurobarometer surveys or
similar polls demonstrates that disinterest in the Community runs much higher than either strong approval or
disapproval.[89] Because massive public support is necessary to bring about a change in the present institution-

al structure, one can expect continued inertia if one
employs a neo-functionalist analysis. What is the problem in all of this if the Community
is functioning well with its present institutions? One
aspect of the problem, a lack of democracy in the Community, will be taken up shortly. Another question, the
effectiveness of current decisional processes, is difficult to answer because there is no other organization
with which to compare the Community. Scheingold observes:

    At present we know very little, if anything, about
    the extent to which weaknesses in the Community po-
    litical system have stood in the way of an indus-
    trial policy and/or the projected transformation
    in business practice.[90]

This problem of institutional development is a
complex one, and it is always easy to criticize with the
wisdom of hindsight. Notwithstanding this, it seems
that those who designed the "Community method" relied
too much on the eagerness of political actors to further
institutionalize the integration project, and too little
on mechanisms built into the Treaty of Rome. Hence,
little of substance has occurred in this area.
    Three "academic" criticisms of this theory have
been explicated. A seemingly conscious decision not to
state the federalist goals of neo-functionalism was the
first. The other two, the problem of engendering spillover and the lack of mechanisms for further institutionalization, are intertwined. If spillover worked according to plan, the Ten would not be in institutional inertia. As noted earlier, these shortcomings in the theory
are important because of their effect on the concrete
reality of the European Community.
    The direct election of the European Parliament,
called for originally in the Treaty of Rome,[91] has not
yet changed the nature of the Community. Full-scale
campaigns, prestigious Members of the European Parliament (MEPs), and intersted publics were hopefully to
give the Community a "shot in the arm" which would spill
over into greater integration. The directly elected
MEPs were expected to be able to generate greater public
support for "European" goals. After four years this has
not occurred, and one must ponder whether the disappointing outcome of the direct elections is not rooted
in the neo-functionalist paradigm.

Ideological Critique

    In order to more fully understand the theoretical
flaws of neo-functionalism, it is necessary to undertake an examination of its political biases. One of
them, a presumption that European politics is non-

ideological, seems worthy of criticism simply because it
is wrong. The other, a tendency to bypass democratic
means of decision-making, may not be a universal political mistake, but it seems ill-suited for the political
culture of western Europe. The first, in a sense, pro-
duces the second: if there is little for a government to
do but discover the most efficient means of administration - all political content having been settled -
democracy may not seem so very important.

Our discussion of neo-functionalist adherence to
"end of ideology" politics will follow two lines of
analysis. The first will be an examination of neo-
functionalist comments on the subject. The second will
be a glance at the contemporary political situation in
the countries of the Ten, and will demonstrate the explanatory failure of the first position.

Most neo-functionalist writing is pitched at a very
high level of abstraction and seldom deals with western
Europe in terms of political particulars. A notable exception is one essay by Ernst Haas, "Technocracy, Pluralism, and the New Europe."[92] This particular article
places in a European context the Haas arguments about
pluralism and the state as a Gesellschaft rather than a
Gemeinschaft. Though it is not recent, it is a superb
example of end of ideology thought popular at the time
of the European Community's founding. Haas makes his
points on this subject with crystal clarity, so he will
be quoted extensively. He first describes the "New
Europe":

> Its main economic component is neither capitalism
> nor socialism: it is industrialism ....Minimum
> standards of consumption are assured as given for
> the entire citizenry. If the market mechanism and
> freely negotiated wage levels fail to attain the
> minima the state intervenes with subsidies, family
> allowances, social security payments, educational
> scholarships and retraining funds.[93]

Because the citizens of this new Europe have satisfied their basic economic needs, all except the marginal
members of society have lost interest in ideology, maintains Haas:

> Ideology has lost its former relevance in the rela-
> tions among workers, industrial managers and mid-
> dle-class professionals. The groups which find it
> difficult to adjust to industrialism are the ones
> for whom ideologies remain important. The lower
> middle-class shopkeepers, artisans and inefficient
> farmers who are hard pressed by the advent of mas-
> sive industrialism and large-scale bureaucratized
> enterprise of all kinds are the consumers of doc-
> trinaire ideology today, whether this be communism

or some form of organic, state-oriented socialism.[94]

Having established to his own satisfaction that
western Europe is post-ideological in its politics, Haas
describes why the Community system of regional government is an appropriate one:

> Few people believe that the existing system of
> regional government ...has any claim to longevity.
> I believe that it does. Because it corresponds to
> the nature of the New Europe, the Europe of adap-
> tive interest groups, bureaucracies, technocrats
> and other units with modest but pragmatic interests
> resembling the traditional nationalism of Gross-
> politik only very remotely, it may well be a real
> system of government rather than a temporary
> style.[95]

This last statement may well be the causal link between how Haas perceives politics in postindustrial societies and how neo-functionalists would design a regional government. If all of Haas' assertions are true,
then participatory democracy is an encumbrance to bureaucrats and ordinary citizens alike. But is Haas
correct? Disregard for a moment the Bader-Meinhoff
group, the Red Brigade, the Provisional I.R.A. They have
existed on the fringe of society. Has western Europe
been free of ideology without them? The evidence is
against Ernst Haas.

A prime example is Margaret Thatcher. She was not
twice elected prime minister on the basis of personality
politics, but because of a well-stated ideology with
which a majority of British voters resonated.[96] She
defeated the opposition on political issues. In British
politics one can also note the strife within the Labour
Party which led to the break off of the right wing and
the formation of the Social Democratic Party. The situation in Italy is clearly different, yet certainly it
is stagnation caused by ideological impasse. In Italy,
as in France, communism is not a fringe movement of so-
cietal dropouts, but a major political force.[97] As for
France, it is difficult to deny that there have been
consistent clear distinctions between the right and the
left throughout the postwar era. One might add the
emergence of the Greens in West Germany and the historic
realignments which took place in France in 1981 and in
Greece in 1982. The evidence is that throughout the
Community the issue in most elections is much deeper
than who will be the most effective administrator of
commonly agreed upon policies.[98]

The ideological issues in contemporary Europe are
not only intranational. There also exists broad and
basic disagreement about the structures of the Commu-

nity. As one transnational group of Socialists put it, "'Europe' is not politically neutral."[99] This organization, Agenor, lays out socialist goals for the Community, and calls for planned economies based on workers' needs, a radical redistribution of income, workers' control of industry, and the "ending of exploitation in the third world," all organized by a democratic Community government.[100] This group is only one example that Europeans are not agreed on Community political or economic goals, but it is sufficient to demonstrate that western Europe has not put ideology behind itself.

If ideological issues remain to be worked out, then there ought to be a substantial place for democracy in the institutions of the Community. At present there clearly is not. The daily decision-making power among the Ten belongs to the Commission, while broad policies are formulated by the Council of Ministers. The Parliament, on the other hand, has only scanty power to monitor these other organs, and no power to originate legislation.[101]

It may be argued that not only is the Community government undemocratic, but membership in the Community significantly curtails the power of democratically elected parliaments in the member countries. Paul Taylor observes:

> An important part of the integration process in this analysis (Neo-functionalism) is the transfer of decision-making powers from the national governments to the European institution, that is, the Commission.[102]

Lindberg's analysis is similar. He explains that decision-making powers transferred to the Community "are being exercised in a complex and amorphous bureaucratic structure in which it is extremely difficult to enforce responsibility and accountability. The national parliaments have been the chief losers."[103]

One might argue that this is an invalid criticism because major policies are set by the Council of Ministers who have been elected by their national parliaments. Erwin Lange, a German Social Democrat and MEP, disagrees with that supposition. It is his contention that over the years of the Community's life the national parliaments have gradually lost control of decisions made by the Council. He explains that even if the Ministers report back, as the Germans do to the Bundestag, there is still no organ in Europe with the power to ratify or reject decisions of the Ministers. His suggested solution is a real European Parliament with the normal prerogatives MPs enjoy over their government.[104]

Is this lack of democracy at the center of the Community truly damaging to Europe? Haas thought not. In discussing the possibility of a stronger Parliament he rgued:

> A priori review, in a setting of inevitable tech-
> nical dominance, may delay the preparation of
> policy but not change its content. Public partic-
> ipation may confuse rather than accelerate inte-
> gration by giving the victims of industrialization
> a European platform.[105]

is faith in the ability of technocrats is not shared by
ll observers, however. One student of the Community's
nstitutions, Gerhard Mally, believes that as techno-
ogical and economic integration increases "the need for
democratic controls over the European technocracy will
become increasingly obvious."[106]

The arguments about democracy in the Community are
largely normative, and though cases can be made for
either democratic or technocratic control, a certain set
of political presuppositions or values underlies each
position. Participatory democracy is a sine qua non
within the western European states which comprise the
Community. The question for the institution's future
is whether the people of Europe wish to continue living
within a regional system which entails "a significant
sacrifice of participatory and egalitarian values."[107]
It is my contention that such a system is incompatible
in the long term with the political cultures of the
countries involved, and that though some of the parties
of the right are comfortable with the economic and political outcomes produced by the present Community
structure, the European left will not wholeheartedly
participate in expanding the Community's areas of competence until democratic control is insured.

CONCLUSION

A recurrent theme of this chapter is that the political presuppositions on which neo-functionalism is
built are of major importance because they have dictated
the original structure of the Community, a structure
which has weaknesses because of the theoretical flaws of
neo-functionalism. At the time of the adoption of the
Treaty of Rome in 1958 it was presumed that neo-functionalism's spillover dynamic would bring about the political integration of the Community's member states,
and would do so through a process of incremental growth
in the power of the central institutions. This gradual
increase in central decision-making power is supposed to
be brought about by national political elites who begin
to perceive the advantages of working together on the
regional level.

In the period of twenty-five years since the ECSC
members formed the Community, there has been some prog-

ress in political integration, although integration has clearly not developed to the point described by Haas as a "new political community." Several questions emerge from a consideration of this reality. First, is the dynamic described by neo-functionalists operating in the Community, albeit slowly? Secondly, is it possible that the uneven progress of political integration has causes which are not explained by neo-functionalism, and in fact operate independently of the structural design of the Community? The answers to these questions are the focus of the remainder of this study.

It is my hypothesis that the neo-functionalist method of political integration is not particularly beneficial in bringing about the uniting of Europe because neo-functionalists and their followers in the Community have not solved the problem of motivating political actors to integrate. An investigation of the first direct elections to the European Parliament will demonstrate a lack of motivation among political elites to seriously contest the election because they had little to gain from the effort. If this can be proven, a major flaw in neo-functionalism will have been documented. This theoretical problem having been demonstrated, it will be possible for students of integration to better understand the kinds of forces which do or do not foster regional political unification.

NOTES

1. Philippe Schmitter, "A Revised Theory of Regional Integration," International Organization 24 (Fall 1970): 838.
2. Ernst Haas, The Uniting of Europe: Political, Social, and Economic Forces, 1950-1957 (Stanford: Stanford University Press, c. 1968), pp. 5 & 15.
3. K.C. Wheare, Federal Government, 4th ed. (New York: Oxford University Press, 1964), p. 15.
4. David Easton, The Political System: An Inquiry into the State of Political Science (New York: Knopf, c. 1953), pp. 129-134.
5. ibid., p. 97.
6. Haas, Uniting of Europe, p. 59.
7. Stuart Scheingold, "Domestic and International Consequences of Regional Integration," International Organization 24 (Fall 1970): 980.
8. Jean Jacques Rousseau, The Social Contract (New York: Macmillan, c. 1947) pp. 26-27.
9. Charles Pentland, International Theory and European Integration (New York: Free Press, c. 1973), p. 66.
10. Paul Taylor, "The Concept of Community and the European Integration Process," Journal of Common Market

Studies 7 (Dec. 1968): 86.
    11. Gerhard Mally, The European Community in Per-
spective (Lexington, Mass.: D.C. Heath, Lexington Books,
c. 1973), p. 28.
    12. David Mitrany, "The Prospect of Integration:
Federal or Functional," Journal of Common Market Studies
4 (Dec. 1965): 124.
    13. Paul Taylor, "The Functionalist Approach to the
Problem of International Order: A Defense," Political
Studies 16 (Oct. 1968): 398. Also see Pentland, European
Integration, p. 70.
    14. Mitrany, "Prospect of Integration," p. 121.
    15. Schmitter, "Revised Theory," p. 854.
    16. Haas, "The Study of Regional Integration: Re-
flections on the Joy and Anguish of Pretheorizing,"
International Organization 24 (Fall 1970): 616.
    17. Mitrany, "Prospect of Integration," pp. 141-
142.
    18. ibid.
    19. Pentland, European Integration, p. 98.
    20. Haas, Beyond the Nation State (Stanford: Stan-
ford University Press, c. 1964), p. 34.
    21. Haas, Uniting of Europe, p. 16.
    22. Personal interview, Luxembourg City, Nov. 18,
1978.
    23. Mally, European Community, pp. 239-240.
    24. Karl Kaiser, "The US and the EEC in the Atlan-
tic System: The Problem of Theory," Journal of Common
Market Studies 5 (June 1967): 392.
    25. Leon Lindberg, "Political Integration as a
Multidimensional Phenomenon Requiring Multivariate
Measurement," International Organization 24 (Fall 1970):
652.
    26. Lindberg, "Decision Making and Integration in
the European Community," International Organization 19
(Winter 1965): 59-60.
    27. See, as an example of this literature, Easton,
A Systems Analysis of Political Life (New York: John
Wiley & Sons, c. 1965).
    28. Taylor, "Concept of Community," p. 87.
    29. Haas, Beyond the Nation State, p. 39.
    30. ibid.
    31. Haas, "Technocracy, Pluralism, and the New
Europe," in J.S. Nye,ed., International Regionalism:
Readings (Boston: Little, Brown, c. 1968), pp. 157-158.
    32. Lindberg, "The European Community as a Politi-
cal System: Notes Toward the Construction of a Model,"
Journal of Common Market Studies 5 (June 1967): 344.
    33. Haas, "Regional Integration," p. 631.
    34. Schmitter, "Revised Theory," p. 841.
    35. J.S. Nye, "Comparing Common Markets: A Revised
Neo-Functionalist Model," International Organization 24
(Fall 1970): 798.
    36. Haas, "Regional Integration," p. 633.

40

37. Nye, "Comparing Common Markets," p. 799.
38. Pentland, European Integration, p. 115.
39. Haas, "Turbulent Fields and the Theory of Regional Integration," International Organization 30 (Winter 1976): 186.
40. Nye, "Comparing Common Markets," p. 817.
41. Haas, "Regional Integration." p. 627.
42. Lindberg and Stuart Scheingold, Europe's Would-Be Polity (Englewood Cliffs, N.J.: Prentice-Hall, c. 1970), pp. 78-79.
43. Nye, "Comparing Common Markets," p. 808.
44. Lindberg and Scheingold, Europe's Would-Be Polity, p. 81.
45. Schmitter, "Revised Theory," p. 864.
46. Nye, "Comparing Common Markets," p. 809.
47. Lindberg, "Decision Making and Integration." p. 78.
48. Taylor, "Concept of Community," p. 95.
49. Haas, "International Integration: The European and the Universal Process," International Organization 15 (Summer 1961): 369.
50. Schmitter, "Revised Theory," pp. 857-858.
51. Haas and Schmitter, "Economics and Differential Patterns of Political Integration," International Organization 18 (Fall 1964): 261.
52. Lindberg, The Political Dynamics of European Economic Integration (Stanford: Stanford University Press, c. 1963), p. 288.
53. Nye, "Comparing Common Markets," p. 822.
54. Haas, "Technocracy, Pluralism," p. 152.
55. Nye, "Comparing Common Markets," p. 799.
56. Haas, "Beyond the Nation State, p. 35.
57. Schmitter, "Revised Theory," p. 865.
58. Nye, "Comparing Common Markets," p. 806.
59. ibid., p. 826.
60. Haas, "Regional Integration," p. 615.
61. Pentland, European Integration, p. 119.
62. Haas, "International Integration," p. 373.
63. Taylor, "Concept of Community," p. 87.
64. Lindberg and Scheingold, Europe's Would-Be Polity, p. 81.
65. Lindberg, "Multidimensional Phenomenon," pp. 649-650.
66. Scheingold, "Domestic and International Consequences," p. 979.
67. Haas, Uniting of Europe, p. 12.
68. Nye, "Comparing Common Markets," p. 805.
69. ibid.
70. Lindberg, "Multidimensional Phenomenon," p. 668.
71. Taylor, "Concept of Community," p. 88.
72. Pentland, European Integration, p. 106.
73. ibid., p. 104.
74. Lindberg, "Multidimensional Phenomenon," p.653.

75. Haas, "Regional Integration," p. 635.
76. ibid.
77. Haas, "Turbulent Fields," p. 183.
78. ibid., p. 175.
79. Haas, "Regional Integration," pp. 639-640.
80. Pentland, European Integration, p. 107.
81. Lindberg, "Integration as a Source of Stress in the European Community System," in Nye, ed., International Regionalism, p. 239.
82. Nye, "Comparing Common Markets," p. 809.
83. Pentland, European Integration," p. 127.
84. Mally, European Community, p. 238.
85. Lindberg, Political Dynamics, p. 286.
86. Lindberg, "European Community as a Political System," p. 348.
87. An example of extra-institutional growth is European Political Cooperation. This effort to unify the foreign policies of the member states is coordinated by the foreign ministers. This group meets at times as the formal Council of Ministers of the European Community. However, when they meet to coordinate external realtions they do so informally. This approach has allowed for the gradual integration of foreign policy, while circumventing the need to amend the Treaty of Rome.
88. Nye, "Comparing Common Markets," p. 802.
89. For example, see Commission of the European Communities, "Euro-Barometer no. 8," (Brussels: Commission of the European Communities, Jan. 12, 1978).
90. Scheingold, "Domestic and International Consequences," p. 987.
91. Treaty of Rome provisions concerning the direct election of the Parliament are contained in Article 138. See A Parliament for Europe (Luxembourg: Secretatiat of the European Parliament, 1978), p. 6.
92. This article, "Technocracy, Pluralism, and the New Europe," which appears in Nye, ed., International Regionalism, pp. 149-176, is the clearest available statement of Haas' own political views and his assessment of politics within the European Community.
93. ibid., p. 155.
94. ibid., p. 156-157.
95. ibid., p. 155.
96. "Britain's Iron Lady," Newsweek (May 14, 1979), pp. 50-59 provides a good discussion of Thatcher's popularity.
97. Victor Leduc, "The French Communist Party: Between Stalinism and Eurocommunism," Political Quarterly 49 (Oct. 1978): 400-410.
98. Eric Shaw, "The Italian Historical Compromise," Political Quarterly 49 (Oct. 1978): 411-424.
99. "The Anti-Tindemans Report," Agenor 57 (Dec. 1975): 5.
100. "Letter to an Anti-Marketeer," Agenor 51 (Spring 1975): 2.

101. For a thorough discussion of powers granted to the Parliament by the Treaty of Rome, see Powers of the European Parliament (London: Information Office of the European Parliament, 1978).

102. Taylor, "Concept of Community," p. 84.

103. Lindberg, Political Dynamics, p. 295.

104. Erwin Lange, MEP, personal interview, Palais de l'Europe, Strasbourg, France, Nov. 15, 1978.

105. Haas, "Technocracy, Pluralism," p. 170.

106. Mally, European Community, p. 131.

107. Scheingold, "Domestic and International Consequences," pp. 997-998.

2
European Socialist Parties
and the Community:
A Historical
and Ideological Overview

Studies of the present must find their context in the past; studies of pragmatic action must draw on the ideologies of the actors. The dynamic history of European socialism, the variety of ways it developed in individual countries, and the political and intellectual trends found in each socialist and social democratic party are all relevant factors in assessing the roles played by these parties in the European Community (EC) and in their relationships with each other. It is the purpose of this chapter to investigate the political and ideological development of the three parties under study in order to make some sense of their actions during the 1979 direct election campaign. Throughout the chapter an attempt will be made to identify both the uniqueness and the commonalities among three socialist parties.

The history of European socialism, though barely a century old (in the sense of the existence of mass-based political parties), is both fascinating and complex. An in-depth analysis of the socialist movement in any one country - let alone three - would be the subject for a book. Hence, the analysis presented here will be limited to those factors which pertain to the relationship of the parties to the European Community. The Social Democratic Party (SPD) of West Germany, the _Parti Socialiste_ (PS) of France, and the British Labour Party will be examined in turn and several questions about each party will be addressed. Specifically, I hope to discover each party's particular orientation toward socialism, its past and present positions on membership in the European Community, and its attitudes toward the European Parliament, its Socialist Group, and the direct elections. It should then be possible to draw a few conclusions and predictions about the functioning of the three parties in any movement toward one integrated Socialist Party of Europe.

One remark about terminology is important. Though the terms "socialist" and "social democrat" are at times defined with differing nuances, and though the parties themselves tend to use one or the other for political reasons, they will be used interchangeably here for any party which belongs to the European Parliament's Socialist Group. Ideological inexactitude can perhaps be excused in the interest of eliminating unnecessary verbiage.

THE SPD: GRASPING THE CENTER

The Sozialdemokratische Partei Deutschland (SPD), though it has enjoyed legitimacy similar to that of the Labour Party in recent decades, differs from the British party in the historical and ideological circumstances of its early years and in its resolutions of the electoral problems of being socialist in the post-World War II era. Perhaps there is a distinctly German national character at the roots of the SPD's ability to conform its practices to its espoused ideology. Whatever the reason, as the German socialists have moved methodically toward the center of the Federal Republic's politics during the past twenty-five years, they have managed to preserve party unity and to transform their ideological statements to conform with their pragmatic actions. They present an interesting case study: Marx's great hope when they were founded, national defenders during World War I, avowed democrats as they attempted to govern Weimar, courageous resisters during World War II, and pragmatic postindustrial politicians since the late 1950s.

The SPD's record vis-à-vis the European Community is a part of the history of its ideological transformation during the 'fifties. For that reason the story of the SPD's efforts to chart a new course for itself is integral to this chapter. Our discussion of the SPD will concentrate on the following topics: founding, organization, socialist ideology, and attitudes on the Community, its Parliament, and the direct elections. Because my purpose here is to lay the groundwork for describing the SPD's role in the 1979 European campaign, the discussion will be limited to pre-1979 developments.

The SPD was founded in 1869, much earlier than the British and French socialist parties. However, as were Labour and the SFIO (Section francaise de l'Internationale ouvriere), it was formed by a coalition of left groups and hence had to deal with ideological and tactical tensions. The principal founder, Wilhelm Liebknecht, was the most radical of the early leaders, but compromise with co-founders Ferdinand Lassalle and August Bebel resulted in a party program somewhat committed to gradualism. Marxist theory predominated, class struggle was affirmed, and the bourgeois state was condemned, but Lassalle's tactics of working for short term reform were adopted in the party's 1875 program.[1]

In 1878 Otto von Bismarck became the major figure
affecting the ideological formation of the SPD. Anti-
socialist legislation enacted that year sererely re-
stricted the party's legal activities. In 1881 Bismarck
adopted a new tactic: a series of welfare measures which
he hoped would lessen the appeal of the Social Democrats. In 1890 he was dismissed, the anti-socialist
laws were repealed, and the SPD emerged stronger, more
united, and distinctly further left than it had been in
1878.[2] Ideological confusion began to prevail again in
the early 1890s. One student of the SPD's ideological
development analyzes the situation thusly:

> Bismarck's policies had forced the party into il-
> legal activity; illegal activity called for more
> revolutionary theory; that theory was adopted at
> the very moment the party was resuming its normal
> political role. The result was the wide disparity
> between theory and practice that characterized the
> SPD until 1959.[3]

Though trade unions were never incorporated into
the SPD as they were into Labour, unionists joined the
party in large numbers in the years around 1900 and
their participation had the same moderating effect as
did the role of the British unions. While Rosa Luxembourg, Karl Kautsky, and Karl Liebknecht urged the party
further left, electoral success depended upon supporting
short term reforms which would better the lives of German workers. As Europeans began preparing for World War
I the workers perceived their economic futures tied to
the success of Germany's imperialistic ventures.[4] The
SPD made a pragmatic choice in 1914, opting for electoral success, and on August 4 the Reichstag delegation
voted unanimously for the war credits bill.[5] The Social
Democrats had chosen the defense of the German state
over universal class struggle.
  Events at the end of the war almost destroyed the
party, and in fact did destroy its left wing. The most
radical leaders were expelled from the SPD in January
1917 for disciplinary reasons, and then founded the Independent Social Democratic Party (USPD). In December
1918 the most revolutionary wing of the USPD broke off
and formed the Communist Party of Germany (KPD). They
attempted a revolution in Berlin in 1919, and the SPD as
part of the governing coalition ordered the Kaiser's
troops to crush them. The government's failure to control the military power they unleashed allowed bloody
excesses, including the murders of Rosa Luxembourg and
Karl Liebknecht.[6]
  During those stormy months the SPD clearly proved
its opposition to violent revolution and its intention
to conduct itself as a mainstream political party. As
Berlau notes, "The SPD, anxious to prevent the success

of the USPD and KDP, had erased all characteristics which clearly distinguished between the SPD and the other parties of the Weimar coalition."[7] As the Weimar Republic came into being the SPD had set its policy in two crucial areas: a commitment to evolutionary socialism through parliamentary means and firm support for the German state. This was not the end of ideological battles within the party, but from this point the tactics of its mainstream never drifted toward anti-democratic measures.

Throughout the Weimar years the SPD continued to espouse Marxist rhetoric, but as a partner in almost every coalition government the party was not able to produce socialist reforms. The following years of the Third Reich were a time of virtual standstill in German political activity. After World War II forces within Germany and beyond the borders of the new Federal Republic had a profound effect on the Social Democrats. The ideological changes the party underwent during the years until the historic Bad Godesberg program was adopted in 1959 altered the basic characteristics of the SPD and provided the ideological underpinnings for its contemporary attitude toward the European Community.

The experience of many SPD leaders who spent the war years in the western democracies, combined with the impact of the partition of the German state and the creation of the German Democratic Republic (GDR), led many in the party toward a harsh view of Stalin's Soviet Union and a cooperative attitude toward the occupation forces in the western sector.[8] These experiences, plus the lesson on an all-powerful state they received during the Nazi years, caused Kurt Schumacher and his colleagues to begin a re-examination of their commitment to Marxism and state control. Furthermore, it was imperative in the European political context of the early cold war for the Social Democrats to clearly distinguish themselves from communism and to broaden their political base if they were to gain electoral success. Schumacher's decision to move the party toward the center was summarized in his stated goal of changing the Arbeiterpartei into a Volkspartei.[9]

After Schumacher's death in 1952 the party leadership was assumed by Erich Ollenhauer who continued support for the project of creating a new party program. The document finally adopted at the Bad Godesberg Conference in 1959 was tantamount to heresy for a Marxist party. The German nation, not the working class, became the prime historical reality; emphasis was placed on the restoration of the German state, not on building a classless society.[10] In fact, this program defines social democracy as a "community of people who come from various schools of belief or thinking," and in enumerating these schools makes no mention of Marxism.[11]

The Bad Godesberg program is still considered the

basic statement of the SPD's goals, but it was followed
in 1975 by a document usually referred to as OR '85
(Orientierungsrahmen - Framework for Orientation).[12]
The drafting of this document and the accompanying ques-
tioning of the meaning of socialism in the Federal Republic were in part initiated by the left wing of the
SPD, many of whom were dissatisfied with the Basic Program of 1959.[13] However, there was little in OR '85 as
it finally emerged to satisfy the desires of the Jusos
(Young Socialists: the party's left wing) and other reformist elements who had hoped for "a novel and integrated approach to the great economic, social, and political problems of the times."[14]
The Framework for Orientation states that:

> The decision for Socialism can have various bases.
> The consensus of democratic Socialists is not root-
> ed in any unitary religious, philosophical or sci-
> entific belief, but rather in common political ob-
> jectives resting on common basic ethical values.
> These basic values are freedom, justice, and soli-
> darity.[15]

It is interesting to note that "equality" is not mentioned and further interesting to read that the values
of democratic socialism "rest on humanistic and Christian tradition."[16] The mainstream SPD has firmly rejected Marx, even as their ultimate philosophical base.
This discussion thus far makes little mention of
discord within the ranks of the SPD. It does exist, and
its major source is debate initiated by the Young Socialists or Jusos. Theoretically this group consists of
all SPD members below age thirty-five, but in 1973 when
they reached the height of their power their actual
strength was estimated at about twenty thousand.[17] The
Jusos, as mentioned above, have been instigators of programmatic debate within the party,[18] but in recent years
their effectiveness has been reduced because of their
own internal conflicts.[19]
The Jusos differ from the Labour left and the CERES
faction of the PS in one major concrete way: they have
not been able to grasp power either within the party organization or in the SPD's Bundestagfraktion (parliamentary delegation). The party, which has close to one
million members, is a highly centralized organization
led by a thirty-six member executive (Parteivorstand)
and an eleven member "inner cabinet" of the executive.
Policy guidelines for the Fraktion are decided by these
groups, and Bundestag committee members report to the
Parteivorstand regularly. There is also a Fraktion-
vorstand (parliamentary executive) which is responsible
for seeing that party decisions are carried out in the
Bundestag.[20] It is a fact of SPD life that these leadership positions are firmly under the control of the

SPD's center and right wings, associated with such figures as Willy Brandt and Helmut Schmidt.[21] Though the
left is present and vocal, its members have not been a-
ble to grasp the power necessary to operationalize their
political goals.

Turning to the SPD's relationship with the European
Community one can expect several things: (1) a shift in
position coinciding with the development of the 1959
Basic Program; (2) the absence of Marxist anti-Community
rhetoric; and (3) the inability of the Young Socialists
to make the impact of their criticism felt.

When the Schuman Plan was introduced in 1951 the
SPD leadership had to reject it for both political and
ideological reasons. Politically, they were the major
opposition party, and ideologically they still stood
firmly against the triple evils of "clericalism, capitalism, and cartels." These two factors, combined
with a strong suspicion of French motives and fears
about the effect of the Plan on the future reunification
of the German state, produced a party position firmly
opposed to the French initiative. The reasoning behind
SPD opposition to the Coal and Steel Community was explained in a 1952 Foreign Affairs article by Carlo
Schmid, one of the party leaders at the time. There
were three lines of attack in the Schmid essay: suspicion that French nationalism was behind the Schuman
Plan, fear that once the Federal Republic joined a western international organization all hopes for German reunification would be gone, and a good deal of antagonism
about the fact that West Germany still did not enjoy
complete freedom in conducting its international affairs. "Since the Federal Republic is only a provisional
arrangement covering one section of a country it cannot
under any condition enter into agreements that would
presume to determine the definitive status of all Germany."[22]

The pragmatism of the post-war SPD is well illus-
trated by their actions once the Federal Republic became
a founding member of the ECSC. Party members took their
assigned places in the Common Assembly, and became one
of the major forces in the formation of the Assembly's
Socialist Group.[23] The Socialists were the first transnational political group to be established, and from the
outset the West Germans took a leadership role within it
and attempted to use it as a forum to advance workers'
rights in Europe.[24] Involvement in the ECSC coincided
with the ideological debate of the mid-fifties, and by
1957 the SPD had changed its position to the extent that
the Bundestagfraktion voted in favor of the Treaty of
Rome without even demanding a roll call.[25]

There are two possible interpretations of these and
other changes brought about by the SPD in the 1950s.
The first is that the SPD was responding to political
realities in a totally opportunistic manner, that is,

because the German people approved of NATO and the Community and held little hope for German reunification, the SPD readjusted as the price of electoral success. The second is that the SPD was responding to political realities in the only way possible: by accepting and working within the politically limiting situation of the Federal Republic at the time. Though one cannot deny that the Social Democrats have abandoned Marxism, even rhetorically, and that they have willingly participated in a coalition government with the Christian Democrats (CDU/CSU), they can also be credited with Ostpolitik, a consistent effort to improve social conditions within the Community, firm positions on European aid to the third world, and, of late, extensive dialogue with several Eurocommunist parties.[26] They are realists and pragmatists, but they retain several commitments which at least identify them as a party of working people, though certainly not a revolutionary organization.

Speaking before the European Parliament in November 1973, Willy Brandt, then Chancellor of the Federal Republic, stated: "Let me now speak on European unification and say something I would not have said in this way ten years ago: we can, and we will, create Europe,... The move toward European union is indispensible."[27] Brandt further explained that by unification he meant "a sensibly organized European government which in the field of common policies will be able to take the necessary decisions and which will be subject to parliamentary control."[28] However, Brandt and his party want to build this united Europe to conform to distinct political views held by the SPD.

The German Social Democrats have taken firm positions on several issues concerning the Community. They include democracy in Community institutions, social policy, enlargement to include Europe's southern tier, foreign aid, and European Political Cooperation. Through examining party statements from the 1960s and 1970s on these matters, it is possible to obtain a clear picture of the mainstream attitude toward membership in the EC. It should be remembered, however, that the Jusos' position is anti-Community largely because they see the EC as an organization dominated by capital, and that their position is not adequately reflected in SPD statements.[29]

In 1977 the Press and Information Office of the Federal Republic published, translated into the major European languages, and distributed a book called Texts Relating to the European Political Co-operation.[30] In this volume the SPD/FDP (Free Democratic Party) government assembled communiques and declarations of the nine foreign ministers dealing with international issues, major speeches before the United Nations and Council of Europe, and statements by the German government. The existence and wide distribution of this document[31] point

to the SPD's commitment to an integrated foreign policy,
as do statements by Schmidt and Brandt contained in the
volume. Schmidt, Federal Chancellor, declared in 1976:

> The European Political Cooperation of recent years
> has proved to be flexible and useful. This co-op-
> eration should be strengthened by a mutual obliga-
> tion on the part of Member States to consult one
> another and the will as a general rule to proceed
> on the basis of the results of such consulta-
> tions.[32]

Statements from SPD party conferences take up the
same theme. The European Committee of the SPD issued a
policy document, "Sozialdemokratische Europapolitik," in
1975, and called firmly for "central decisionmaking
authority in the area of foreign and defense policy."[33]
The specific policies which the SPD wants taken up by
the Community are explicated in this same document. A
social democratic orientation for European foreign policy is viewed as a means to strengthen the developing
world and reduce its direct dependence on the indus-
trialized nations.[34] Two further SPD goals are to
"halt the use and threat of power as a political means"
and to further "European integration, the Atlantic alliance, increased cooperation between the East and West
and between the European Community and the Third
World."[35] These policies which the SPD wishes placed on
the EC's agenda are basic to the Social Democrats' sense
of the Federal Republic's role in international affairs.
The adoption of these positions by the Community would,
in their analysis, strengthen Europe as a third force in
world affairs: "The SPD seeks to promote European economic and political integration because it would ideally
like to see Europe become a more independent force in
international politics."[36] There is German self-interest involved here, but views on détente, disarmament,
and relations with the less developed countries (LDCs)
are significantly to the left of prevailing American
and right wing European positions.

Reform of Community institutions has been a long
term and consistent issue for the SPD. In 1965 the
party's shadow cabinet issued a statement on European
policy which declared:

> The democratic element in the European Community is
> too small. National parliaments are losing rights
> which are not handed over to the European Parlia-
> ment. The Social Democratic Federal Government
> will work for the grant of the classical rights and
> duties of a democratic legislature to the European
> Parliament.[37]

The idea of giving substantive power to the Parliament,

and particularly not increasing central authority by the
alternative of new grants of power to the Commission,
has been advanced by the SPD more than by any other party of the large nations of the EC. In 1975, one of the
four specific goals supported by the Social Democrats
for the Community was that "The European Community must
expand to a federal European Union with democratic institutions."[38] This goal was to be set in motion by a
three step plan.[39] Step one includes seven specific
provisions for transferring rights lost by the national
parliaments to the European Parliament. Chief among
these is additional power to control the Community budget.[40] The second step is the direct election of the
Parliament, a move also advocated in the 1965 policy
statement.[41] Third, the SPD recommended that the Parliament and Council be equal in legislative power.[42]
These reforms, if all were enacted, would substantially
change the character of the European institutions.

The SPD caused at least one brief political furor
in Europe because of these positions. In autumn 1978
Helmut Schmidt publicly declared his hopes that the
directly elected Parliament would obtain substantive
powers. Giscard d'Estaing, with whom Schmidt usually had
a cordial, cooperative relationship, delivered a major
address stating France's opposition to any such idea.
For several days the European press hummed with the dispute.[43] However, the SPD still attempts to keep a
pledge made by Brandt: "Nothing must keep us from pro-
gressively adding to the responsibilities of the European Parliament. Its powers must be widened."[44] In
fact, the SPD leadership is fond of recalling that its
1925 Heidelberg program called for a "United States of
Europe" with a directly elected legislature.[45]

Broad concerns about regional, social, and economic
policy, and rights of women, children, and workers form
another major plank of the SPD's position on the Community. Though the party never espouses a Marxist position on these issues, the Social Democrats make every
attempt to make the solution of these problems a higher
priority for the EC than it has been. "For too long we
have allowed social policy to be a mere appendix to
competition," said Brandt in a typical SPD statement.[46]
In 1977 a party declaration listed eight issues which
the SPD believes no European state can solve in isolation. Among them are rising unemployment, controlling
the power of multinational corporations, and realization
of a regional policy in Europe to end north-south dis-
parities.[47]

Concerning enlargement of the Community, the entire
Socialist Group took the same favorable position during
the 1970s, albeit for different reasons. Labourites
are frank in stating that they hope enlargement will
slow down integration,[48] whereas the German position
seeks to conclude the era of the Community as a "rich

man's club." In 1965 the party leadership declared,
"The interests of the German people are not served by a
community of EEC member states which is protectionist,
introverted, and complete in itself."[49] OR '85 recalls
that today's economic difficulties do not call for a
"new isolationism, but rather the continuing attempt to
improve the ability to function and suitable expansion
of international organisations."[50]

The SPD's position on the Community have been both
coherent and consistent for the past twenty years. They
can be summarized as democracy, social equality, open-
ness to the developing world, and the creation of "Europe" as an independent international force. It is not
a blind affirmation of the Community which the SPD has
developed, but an attempt to make their particular type
of social democracy a major factor in European politics:

> Our policy of reform must therefore be aimed at Eu-
> rope as a whole. This presupposes at the same time
> that the forces of Democratic Socialism in Europe
> and their allies develop a common policy for Eu-
> rope. The German Social Democratic movement is un-
> der a special obligation in this.[51]

In terms of practical politics during the Brandt -
Schmidt era, the leadership of the SPD experienced little disagreement on Community policy. Though Brandt
possesses a "style of describing the European future in
very evocative terms,"[52] the center and right of the SPD
agreed on most substantive issues. However, one factor
must be kept in mind when assessing the practical performance on Community-related issues of the SPD's recent chancellors: they functioned in coalition governments, and though they were the senior partner the post
of foreign minister was held by the Free Democrats
(FDP). This situation combined with practical political
exigencies did at times create a breach between the party's idealized construct of Europe and the short term
policies pursued by West Germany in the Council of Ministers.[53] For example, Schmidt, though he bore responsibility for the coalition's day to day policies, was
also the person who authored the statement on Europe
in OR '85 which is quoted above.[54] The SPD, in terms of
being able to stand united behind a coherent policy, has
been far more fortunate than Labour or the French Socialists. However, their British and French colleagues
are possibly far more invigorated and challenged by the
debates which often rage within their parties.

In summary, the leadership of the SPD has been successful in the past twenty-five years in changing its
image in the minds of German voters. It has become the
Volkspartei envisioned by Schumacher, though in the process it has lost much of the richness of its history.
Its European policy is a faithful reflection of its

opes for the Federal Republic: a democratic political
tructure with a strongly humanitarian social policy.
hough the minority position of the Jusos very often
recludes significant policy clashes, which mav be a
eakness, the strength of the SPD's position is that
hey are the most unified and pro-European of the three
ajor parties in the Socialist Group. If any of these
arties was in a position to foster united socialist
ction in the 1979 campaign, it was the Social Democrats
f West Germany.

HE PARTI SOCIALISTE: THE CONSTRAINTS
F COALITION

French socialists have historically been "good
uropeans." The Section francaise de l'Internationale
uvriere (SFIO), France's pre-1970 socialist party, was
coalition partner in the French government which nego-
iated the Treaty of Rome. Today's Parti Socialiste
PS) continues to support the Community insofar as it
ay become a "Europe of the workers."[55] However, until
he historic elections of 1981 French socialists oper-
ted within a political system which placed considerable
onstraints on both their ideological and tactical free-
om: politicos and political scientists alike presumed
hat no French party would be able to govern the Fifth
epublic without a coalition partner. During the Fourth
epublic the SFIO participated in center coalitions. In
he 1970s the PS - in or out of the Common Program -
eemed to have no choice but to throw its lot with the
ommunists (PCF). Because this was a political reality
t the time of the first direct election, as one ex-
mines the development of the Socialist Party's posi-
ions on the Community it is necessary to weigh the role
f the PCF in helping to form these positions.
    The Socialist Party - even without considering
heir sometimes allies, the PCF - has at least three ma-
or ideological trends within it, and among these fac-
ions there is spirited debate about the proper social-
st role in European integration. When this internal
onflict is added to PCF hostility toward the Community
t becomes evident that the European policy of the PS
as a delicate affair during the years leading up to the
979 election. In order to place the party in a context
o discuss its European election campaign, it is impor-
ant not only to examine its "European" history, but
lso to investigate how the change in the direction in
hich it moved to seek a coalition partner, and the
alancing required to maintain a relationship with the
CF while trying to strengthen itself, affected the PS's
uropean policies prior to 1981.
    The French Socialist Party (SFIO) was formally
ounded in 1905 when two factions, the Guesdist and

Jauresian, were able to achieve a unity of ideology and tactics.[56] The two factions represented the classic tension in socialism: the Guesdists were Marxist and revolutionary in their orientation, while the Jauresians were utopian socialists with reformist and republican tendencies.[57] The two groups were able to come together temporarily in 1896 through agreement on the Saint-Mande Program authored by Millerand. What he designed was a minimum program "whose acceptance was binding on whoever claimed the title of Socialist."[58] The program had three major elements: its basis was collectivism, "the progressive socialization of the means of production, exchange and distribution;" this was combined with democratic tactics for achieving socialist goals, and international collaboration with militants in other countries.[59] Even though Guesde and his followers accepted this program and joined in the creation of the SFIO, the reformist versus revolutionary tension was strong in French socialism from the outset.

The ideological tension within the party exploded at the Congress of Tours in 1920. On that occasion over two-thirds of the party members quit and founded the French Communist Party.[60] After this event the Socialists, during both the 1920s and the Popular Front era, moved into a position they occupied well into the Fourth Republic as the left party in a coalition with the Radicals. They became, and one might argue they still are, a party with a bifurcated sense of themselves. They began to make inroads into Radical electoral strongholds as they strengthened their republican tendencies, but they were not able to give up their old symbols or Marxist rhetoric.

It was this ambiguity and ambivalance of orthodox princlples and reformist leadership - of class-war dogma and faith in liberal democracy; of opposition to the bourgeois regime and cooperation with the bourgeois parties; of internationalism and patriotism; of revolution and peaceful change - that gave the SFIO a confused sense of mission and a blurred electoral appeal.[61]

The facts of French political life which forced the SFIO into the role of an ideological Janus during the interwar period continued to limit the party's options after liberation. Both the socialists and the communists emerged stronger after the war, but the SFIO was uninterested in unification of the two major left paries. Guy Mollet, party leader from 1946 to 1969, began his first term as general secretary with intentions of forging links with the PCF, but "after the Czech coup, changed his mind and the party began to build on a resolute but sterile anti-communism."[62] The decision to reject an alliance with the communists gave the social-

ists only one other electoral option, and throughout the
Fourth Republic the SFIO participated in coalitions
which attempted to defend the center against extremists
of both left and right.[63]
There was another possible strategy which became
appealing after de Gaulle's triumph in the Fifth Republic: to unite and strengthen the non-communist left,
presuming communist electoral cooperation. Francois
Mitterrand, leader of the Convention des Institutions
republicaines (CIR), was the politician most closely
associated with this strategy.[64] In 1969 the SFIO began
a major process of reorganization which incorporated
the tactics proposed by Mitterrand. The party changed
its name to the "New Socialist Party," and later to its
current name, the Parti Socialiste. Francois Mitterrand
was elected general secretary in 1971, and began the
task of building a successful party from members of the
SFIO, CIR, and several smaller groups.[65]
The 1970s are the most important years for consideration in this study for the obvious reason that they
have the most bearing on the direct election, but also
because it was throughout this decade that the PS looked
to the left for a coalition partner. Four aspects of
the PS during the 1970s will be surveyed: its leadership, its interpretation of socialism, a profile of its
membership, and its participation in the Programme
commun du gouvernement.
The PS is organized in a manner which officially
recognizes factions or tendances.[66] Of these, three are
of major importance here. Mitterrand leads the center
of the party which has continued to be the majority.
There is a strong left - the centre d'études, de recher-
ches et d'éducation socialistes (CERES) - which com-
prises about twenty-five to thirty percent of the party
membership.[67] CERES was at one time led by Michel
Rocard, a former Left-Socialist (PSU). Of late Rocard
has moved toward the party's right and, in the eyes of
some observers, has been anxious for an opportunity to
take over Mitterrand's role as party leader.[68] There is
also a small tendance to the right of the party composed
of Guy Mollet's followers, but there are no serious bids
for party leadership among this group.
The ideology of the party and its leaders must be
viewed not only theoretically, but in terms of practical
and tactical considerations. Mitterrand, for example,
has had to contend with responsibility to hold the party
together, to increase its membership, to achieve success
at the polls, and meanwhile to ward off challenges to
his leadership. One observer finds that both Mitterrand
and Rocard are "realists about what can be changed, what
is likely to be changed, and what the changes are going
to cost French society."[69] In fact, this writer, William Pfaff, sees the major division in French socialism
as one between the pragmatists and the visionaries, and

56

contends, "In this division, Mitterrand and Rocard are on the same side, pragmatists both, as against those who believe in the possibilities of radical and even redemptive transformation of French society."[70] Criticism that the PS has had too strong a visionary element has been offered by both British and German socialists who smart at French accusations that they have abandoned Marxism, and who have retaliated with the claim that their Gallic colleagues would quickly lose their idealism in government.[71] During the 1970s, the leadership of the PS had to contend with both the pragmatists and the idealists, and meanwhile position itself so as to win an election.

Francois Mitterrand discussed his views on social democracy and Marxism in an interview with l'Express in 1978. He spoke, first of all, of "l'éternel dilemme" of socialists: whether to attempt revolutionary breaks in the social fabric or to work "by patience and tenacity for successive transitions."[72] He then described the social structure he envisioned, and one senses that he was walking a tightrope. He wanted to enlarge the "range of the public sector." However, "We do not intend to suppress the market economy, as in the collectivist countries, but to subordinate its orientations and decisions to a democratic plan."[73] At the end of the interview he described socialism as the "freedom to be oneself,"[74] but at the same time professed that he was not ready to move the PS to a position similar to that adopted in the SPD's Bad Godesberg program.[75] One finds the pre-1981 Mitterrand taking positions which are understandable for a leader of a fragile coalition - the PS - who would like to enlarge its base by taking on even more squabbling members.

Michel Rocard has been the champion of one French socialist idea in particular: autogestion (self-management). This position is seen by some CERES socialists and by the PCF leadership as opposed to nationalization and centralized planning.[76] It is certainly, as will be discussed below, a position which makes it difficult to work for centralized planning at the Community level. However, it is an idea very much in accord with the humanist and personalized strand of French socialism.

What is socialism in contemporary France? It is an amalgam of strains of leftist thinking. To use Millerand's method of minimalist definition, it is democratic, reformist, humanistic, anti-Soviet, anti-imperialist. It favors a mixed economy and in its ranks there exists considerable sympathy for local control. Any more precise a definition would leave out substantial currents of thought within the Socialist Party.

Who is socialist in France? David Bell notes, "The new Parti Socialiste is still middle-class but represents those sectors of the middle-class which are politically left-wing."[77] In 1975 only three percent of the members were workers and seven percent employees (sixty percent of the PCF members are workers). The majority of party activists are urban and educated, many of them liberal professionals and teachers. The kind of membership the PS attracted throughout the 1970s created another dilemma: should party leaders move toward luring new working class members from the ranks of the CGT , or try to increase their hold on the educated, young middle class, or attempt to gain on both flanks?

After the party's 1971 Congress the PS attempted to form a potential government coalition with the PCF. The Programme Commun, signed in 1972 after intensive negotiations between the PS and PCF, held together for five years. In the summer and fall of 1977, amidst hopes for a left victory in the parliamentary elections of March 1978, the two parties attempted to work out specific programs and ministerial positions for a future coalition government. By September 1977 conflicts caused this round of negotiations to be halted, and although they were resumed a few weeks later, by mid-November the left alliance was totally in ruins. The Common Program held together for five years, most likely because it was vague on issues of potentially substantial disargeement, but unity between the PS and PCF crumbled when concrete issues were at stake and electoral victory seemed imminent.[78] The original Common Program articulated a call for numerous practical reforms in economic, political, and international spheres. Among them were:

> broadening of trade unions' power of co-determination within firms; nationalization of the most important economic sectors...; vague calls for a 'more democratic' state economic planning and direction; doing away with the primacy of the President;...renunciation of strategic nuclear weapons ... and the full independence of France from any politico-military bloc.[79]

Though the Union of the Left crumbled as its critical test approached, and although the PS and PCF planned to run separately in the European elections and the 1981 presidential election, in 1978 Mitterrand was still maintaining that "The Parti Socialiste remains faithful to the commitments of the Common Program."[80]

Before moving to a discussion more directly relevant to the European Community, we must pull several strands together. First is the historical irony that the same effort to unite revolutionary and reformist elements of the left at the turn of the century has continued to be an issue in French politics. It seems that the French left cannot succeed divided, but neither can they succeed in staying united. The second important observation is that the PS has a distinctly different membership than do the SPD and Labour. In France there

is a viable alternative further to the left, and the
majority of workers have opted for it in most recent
elections (It must be remembered that the 1981 election,
which may signal a critical realignment of the working
class, had no bearing on strategies employed for the
first European elections). The third, and perhaps most
important observation is that politics in France exists
in a state of flux, so what seems to be the course plot-
ted by a particular party or politician can change
rapidly.

The French Socialist Party's views on the European
Community will be discussed along the same lines as
those of their German colleagues. A brief historical
survey will be followed by an examination of contemporary positions on several key issues. Broadly speaking,
the PS and its predecessors have been pro-Europe parties, which seems appropriate for socialist parties
which have taken internationalism seriously since their
founding. However, this basic disposition does not mean
that the PS, particularly the CERES faction, has been
without hard questions and well-grounded opposition to
European integration as it has thus far developed.

In December 1951 the French National Assembly ratified the Treaty of Paris establishing the ECSC. The
largest pro-European bloc in the Assembly was the SFIO
which contributed 105 affirmative votes.[81] Though the
party gave firm support to functionalism as a method of
achieving European federation, its leadership was dissatisfied with two aspects of the Schuman Plan: the absence of Great Britain from the original Six and the
lack of a democratically elected assembly to which the
functional institutions would be responsible.[82] In 1949
the party's congress had taken up the issue of integration along the lines proposed by Foreign Minister Schuman, and their official reaction called for certain
conditions: workers' representatives on the High Authority, a responsible European Assembly, and the membership
of as many European nations as possible. One student of
the period notes: "Each of these conditions expressed
different aspects of the SFIO's tradition: its socialism, its profound belief in popular sovereignty, its
'French' fear of Germany and its idealistic regard for
Britain."[83]

France's 1956 elections brought a "pro-Europe"
government to power with Guy Mollet as premier. The
Mollet government led France through the Treaty of Rome
negotiations and Mollet himself argued strenuously for
the formation of the European Economic Community. In-
terestingly, he proposed "a political, rather than an
economic defense of the Treaties;"[84] that is, he attempted to make his colleagues understand that France by
itself simply could not be a major international force.
The socialists of the late 1950s and 1960s continued to
be firmly pro-Community under Mollet's leadership. How-

ever. their integrationist stance had only a very insig-
nificant socialist content.

Guy Mollet, along with a few other European politicians like Henri Spaak of Belgium, devoted much of his
own career and his party's energy to European integration. In 1966 when he had been Secretary General of the
SFIO for twenty years, le Monde conducted a lengthy interview about Europe with him. At the time he identi-
fied three European issues on which the French parties
disagreed, and which he contended would shape alliances
for the next French election. They were transfer of
sovereignty versus nationalism, political democracy versus current EC structures, and socialism versus liberalism in economic policy. As he discussed these three
choices and the positions of the Federation of the
Socialist and Democratic Left (FGDS) in contrast to the
conservatives, liberals, and communists, the difficult
position of the socialists became clear. Whereas they
and the liberals wers supporters of supranationality,
the PCF certainly was not. However, in regard to economic policy, the FGDS was much closer to the PCF position.[85]

The problem of socialist - communist attitudes on
the Community is well documented in a joint declaration
issued by the FGDS and PCF in February 1968.[86] The
statement begins by setting forth their differences.
The FGDS favored "enlarging Europe territorially...,
increasing the number of common sectors... and setting
up a common political authority embracing a Parliament
elected by universal suffrage." The PCF, on the other
hand, stated:

> The PCF reaffirms its hostility to the setting up
> of a supranational authority created and dominated
> by capital, as it would accentuate the division of
> Europe, aggravate the baneful consequences for the
> workers of the present policy of the Common Market,
> and leave the democratic policy the French people
> want to the mercy of reactionary foreign govern-
> ments.

Having set forth their differences, the two groups added
three areas of agreement on the Six, "a reality... dominated by cartels, trusts, and international pressure
groups." They agreed that the Community needed to de-
mocratize its technocratic institutions, to give rights
in the Community institutions to industrial and agricultural unions, and to allow all political parties represented in their national parliaments to be represented
in Europe (At the time there were no communists in the
European Parliament).

As one reads the positions of the PCF in contrast
to those of the socialists, the attitudes seem to line
up not so much as a left - right dichotomy, but rather

60

as pessimism versus optimism. Criticisms of the Community's status quo are very similar. However, the French communists seem to have the perception that the Community is hopelessly bound to capitalism and technocracy; the socialists on the other hand seem to see economic and political necessity in remaining a part of Europe, and are therefore willing to put some effort into reforming the Community.

This socialist attitude of 1968 remained the basic orientation of the PS throughout the 1970s, though allegiance to the Common Program from 1972 to 1977 required a certain vagueness in public statements. The PS majority opposed the "creation of a European super-state which will be built on the foundations of neo-capitalism and technocracy."[87] At the same time the PS leadership held to the idea of socialist internationalism and preferred attempts to reform the Community to French isolation. Reform had both global and European dimensions. The PS favored a Community committed to a foreign economic policy of greater cooperation with COMECON (the east European trade association) and restructured trade relations with the third world. Within the Nine the Socialist Party continued to argue for democratic planning and objectives whose purposes are broader than "extracting capitalism from a difficult situation."[88]

Michel Rocard expressed his views on French socialism and Europe in a 1977 Foreign Affairs article. The Community as a comfortable home for multinational corporations came under attack:

> The EEC has, above all, allowed multinational corporations to conduct, in all states where they have located, centralized business practices consisting of, for example: blackmail based on employment, pressure and corruption à la Lockheed, brakes put on policies for regional development, monetary speculation, domination of entire economic sectors of a country - such is the balance sheet of the capitalist integration that has occurred to the detriment of the economic and technological independence of the countries of the EEC.[89]

The predominant role of big business in the Community was singled out for criticism in a November 1978 PS statement on the upcoming direct elections:

> Since, however, capitalist exploitation is increasingly organized on an international scale, and since in the face of this threat the solidarity of those affected is beginning to take on an international dimension, the Socialist Party considers that the fight it is conducting in our country must inevitably be extended to Europe.[90]

As these two statements indicate, the French Socialist Party has taken a strong anti-capitalist stance,
yet they are well aware that the MNCs, whether American
or European, cannot be controlled without a European
Community, albeit one which is greatly modified. In
this, the PS takes a position which differs from the PCF
and the Labour left, who see the EC as hopelessly unre-
formable. However, the question of how to reform the
Community and when to do so is still a difficult problem
for the PS. Essentially, the issue is whether it is
wise to strengthen the European institutions while the
governments of the member states are predominantly in
pro-capitalist hands. In the 1970s this was a particularly burning issue where France itself was concerned.

In 1973 Mitterrand stated that the PS approved of
"all extension of the competence and common responsibilities" of the Community, but then added, "European construction cannot be separated from the willingness to
build Socialism in France."[91] Rocard struck an even
stronger note in 1977. Though he affirmed that the EC's
problems "have not sapped the socialist will to build
Europe," he added, "What the French Socialists want to
do is to build in France a socialist society that will
lead them to pose the problem of a widening of their
struggle on a European scale."[92] It is interesting to
note here that the PS had a hopefulness about their
ability to create a socialist France, an idea which the
Germans seem to have lost and the British may never have
possessed. There seemed to be serious doubt on the part
of the PS concerning their freedom to restructure France
in the future if the Community attained more power before they were able to do so. As Rocard observed: "It
is true that the domination of German and American capital over several important branches of our economy...
does have the effect of reducing our margin of maneuver
for a leftist experiment in France."[93]

Despite some reluctance, particularly on the part
of CERES, the PS gave support to the first direct elections. In 1978 M. Edgar Pisani, MEP, found the election
of the Parliament to be a good thing for three reasons:
(1) it would enhance citizens' understanding that
"Europe is becoming the framework of our life;" (2) it
would place the Parliament's budgetary power under democratic control; and (3) directly elected MEPs would
strengthen the prestige of the Socialist Group and
thereby help them to develop a Euro-socialist view.[94]
In the party's European election manifesto "better
democratic control of Community life, and greater participation by the working world in the decision-making
process" were called for.[95] However, the PS declined to
endorse any grant of powers not designated in the Treaty of Rome to the Community until "the EEC adopted the
aims set out in this Manifesto."[96] Once again, the
future of socialism in France was being protected.

Though the Common Program was formally defunct by 1979, the PS still claimed allegiance to its ideals. In regard to the Community, the program made two major points which seem to be contradictory. On the one hand, the PS - PCF alliance would "participate in building the EEC, its institutions, its common policies, with the will to act in order to free it from the domination of large capitalist enterprise."[97] However, at the same time the coalition would preserve its

freedom of action to implement its own political, economic and social programs domestically. Notably, the government would reserve its right to invoke the protective clauses of the Treaty of Rome if Community decisions conflicted with domestic priorities.[98]

This position is a strong reflection of CERES' doubts about the Community putting a brake on the development of socialism in France, but it is considerably milder in tone than PCF statements since the demise of the Common Program.

The PS presented an interesting yet complex profile as its members prepared for the direct elections. The party seemed more Marxist in its orientation than its British and German colleagues, perhaps because the French Socialist Party had not been exposed to the moderating effects of governing since the founding of the Fifth Republic. The PS contained several strains of attitudes toward integration, but all factions supported in principle the building of Europe. The central question for the party was whether to withhold support from any moves to strengthen the central institutions until the left was in control of France and a majority of the other member states. One point which was clearly not a divisive issue within the PS was the necessity of the existence of some kind of European structure to contain and eventually reform capitalism. Because of the difficult strategic and tactical issues inherent in their efforts to build socialism on both national and regional levels, the French socialists have been simultaneously critics and supporters of the Community.

France's European election of 1979 was conducted by proportional representation, and the PS and PCF made no attempts to collaborate. Though this left the Parti Socialiste theoretically free to wage the campaign its way, the constraints of coalition and the perceived necessity of an alignment with the PCF or the center parties in the next national election meant that the party could not, in any then foreseeable situation, bring its vision of socialism to France or to Europe without compromise. In the 1984 campaign the PS may be much more able to articulate its own distinct vision of a united Europe.

THE LABOUR PARTY: IDEOLOGICAL AND
POLITICAL CONFUSION

The British Labour Party was the last of the members of the Socialist Group participating in the 1979
direct election to send a delegation to the European
Parliament, doing so in 1975, two years after the British Conservatives. These junior members of the Socialist Group are nevertheless of pivotal importance to the
future integration of the Community, though perhaps
their importance will consist of being one of the major
roadblocks to this process. The testiness of Labour's
leadership in regard to Europe is a well known reality,
but not necessarily one amenable to simplistic explanations. An understanding of Labour policies on the Community requires first at least a brief look at the party's structure and history, an exploration of what socialism means to Labour, and an evaluation of the role
of pragmatic concerns in shaping Labour's policy.
Against this backdrop it will be possible to examine
Labour's role during the turbulent period of British
entry negotiations, the most pertinent positions of pro-
and anti-Marketeers, and the alignments on Community issues among party leaders as they approached the direct
election.
    The founding of the Labour Party was an outgrowth
of the enfranchisement of working class males in 1867
and the formation of the Trades Union Congress in 1868.
During the later years of the nineteenth century working
men elected to the House of Commons cooperated with the
Liberals and were thus dubbed "Lib-Labs." Paul Adelman,
a historian of the party's founding, recalls that
Engels, who was furious at their complacency, referred
to them as "'the tail of the great Liberal Party.'"[99]
    Concurrent with this embryonic labor representation
in Parliament, middle class English intellectuals
founded several socialist societies. However, the
idealistic and often brilliant members of such groups as
the Fabian Society and the Social Democratic Foundation
had little interest in practical politics. But by the
turn of the century the union movement had grown and in
the early 1900s the unionists and intellectuals entered[100]
into a marriage of convenience in the Labour Party.
The contrast between the two groups who founded the party is one reason for ideological tension which exists to
this day. Bernard Crick notes that the brains of the
early party were frankly socialist, but the power belonged to the trade unionists who were "always more interested in practical reforms than in social revolution." [101]
    The Labour Party's decision-making structure is an
outgrowth of its initial composition and its extra-
parliamentary founding. Overall party policies, election manifestos and the like are drawn up by the Na-

tional Executive Committee (NEC) which is elected by and reports to the Party Conference. The labor unions wield block votes in Conference; in fact the two largest unions have nearly one-fourth of the total votes.[102] This power was initially given to the unions "to save them from middle-class socialist enthusiam and to ensure their ability to pursue their industrial ends." [103] It means to this day that the NEC is heavily dominated by union leaders and that the positions of the party must reflect the political views of the working class if it is to be successful at the polls.

The Parliamentary Labour Party (PLP) is composed of all Labour MPs, and - especially before the turmoil of 1980-1981 it developed a good deal of independence from NEC policy over the years. [104] Though the Parliamentary Party and the NEC have agreed on most issues, it is possible for the General Secretary of the Labour Party to adhere to a position agreed upon by the NEC while the Prime Minister and the Cabinet lead the PLP in an opposite direction. The potential for fractious behavior is enormous, as can be amply demonstrated by investigating Labour's actions in regard to the Community.

A minor example is British representation to the Confederation of Socialist Parties of the European Community: though there have been pro-Europe MPs in Labour's delegation to the European Parliament who work constructively in the Socialist Group, the NEC chooses delegates to the Confederation of Socialist Parties. Lord Wayland Kennet, MEP, remarked about the Confederation that "None of us (pro-Europe MEPs) go to their meetings because the Confederation is a direct interparty organization. The 'antis' in the Labour Party wouldn't let us near it." [105] Because, as Kennet further notes, "The NEC does not approach the Confederation with good will," [106] European Socialists are confronted with two faces of the Labour Party, one in the Socialist Group and the other in the Confederation.

The structure of the party, whether viewed as problematic or invigorating, is only one source of friction. Another is the historical dichotomy between the Party's stated concept of socialism and Labour's actual purposes and tactics. The Labour Party's Constitution, written in 1918, stated as one of the Party's primary goals, "To secure for the workers by hand or by brain the full fruits of their industry and the most equitable distribution thereof that may be possible, upon the basis of common ownership of the means of production, distribution and exchange."[107] Though this certainly sounds like socialism, and though it is adhered to rhetorically, Samuel Beer contends that the importance of this commitment was not its Socialist stance, but the fact that it signaled Labour's intention to be independent of the Liberals.[108] He also concludes that "At its foundation the party was, and during its later history it remained, massively devoted to parliamentary and democratic methods."[109] Thus, the history of Labour's actions differs from the written record of its philosophy - a situation which creates the opportunity for constant debate about the meaning of British socialism.

The German and French socialist parties were founded on a Marxist ideology with clear revolutionary goals,[110] but this was not the case in Britian. One student of the Labour Party makes a distinction between "democratic socialism" and "social democracy." He observes that the early SPD practiced democratic socialism, that is, the party had clear revolutionary goals, but used parliamentary tactics. On the other hand social democracy actually means:

A form of politics or economic organization that does not envisage, or indeed intend, the achievement of socialism in a future however distant. Whether or not ideologically congenial, it is surely an accurate enough description of the reality in Britain where, its occasional ritualistic pretensions notwithstanding, the Labour Party cannot be said seriously to be an instrument for socialism.[111]

The supposition that British socialism, as embodied in the Labour Party, is distinct from the continental variety is shared by both political scientists and Labour activists. One observer notes that the Labour Party has a "close affinity . . . with traditions of national culture" which has been bolstered by the party's "tardy birth, the lack of class struggle ideology, and a historical period of conflict with state and society."[112] He further contrasts the federal nature of the Labour Party structure in which "groups did not relinquish their own identity or affiliation" with the structure of the German party which was organized at the outset through local party cells joined by individuals.[113]

Though scholars will note ideological and historical difference in a somewhat detached way, some British politicians tend to find another set of differences which of course make their "brand" of socialism superior to that of their European colleagues. Michael Foot, speaking for the NEC at the Party's Common Market Conference in 1975, pointed out that European socialists have often entered into coalition governments and that "very few of them can say that they can secure independent Socialist power" whereas Labour can say "We shall have no truck with any coalition government."[114] This argument and variations on it are frequently used by those Labour Party members opposed to the granting of additional powers to the European Parliament.[115] Baron Edward Castle, a Labour delegate to the European Parliament for several years, comments that the British concept of socialism is non-doctrinaire, but that Labour is further to the left that the SPD in particular.[116] In other words, collaboration with the SPD would retard the growth of socialism in Britain.

It is difficult to grasp what socialism means to the Labour Party without giving due weight to the unions. They, as noted, wield significant power in the Party. They also identify it, according to Peter Jenkins, as "their party" whose purpose is "to assist in or, at the very least, refrain from in any way obstructing the practice of trade unionism."[117] To a significant portion of the Labour Party socialism translates pragmatically into what seems to be good for trade union members. Interest is more important than ideology. Therefore, political rhetoric to the contrary notwithstanding, the Labour Party's mass membership is committed to the policies perceived to be most likely to meet the "bread and butter" needs of British workers. Internationalism and social revolution are not serious goals for most of the NEC. Pragmatic social democracy is the order of the day.

In discussing Labour's tumultuous history vis-à-vis the European Community it should be kept in mind that the party's aims are not primarily international socialist solidarity, but are designed to retain the loyalty of British trade unionists upon whom Labour depends for both financial and electoral support. Added to this factor one can find more than a trace of British elitism and scorn for continental politics. However, it should be noted that a significant minority of party leaders, Labour MPs, and several Ministers have been outspoken advocates of British membership in "Europe." Pro-Market forces were stronger during the 1979 campaign than they are today, owing to the split which resulted in the formation of the Social Democratic Party. Most notably, former European Commissioner Roy Jenkins is not longer a Labour member.

The European Community has been a difficult issue in British politics since the early 1960's, though it has never gained attention as the overriding issue in any election. Peter Byrd analyzes it as a unique conflict for the party because it is a matter of foreign policy which is also enmeshed in practical economic concerns such as food prices. He contends that:

> For the electorate as a whole the issue has certainly appeared to be less important than prices or industrial relations, but it is equally more important than previous disagreements about foreign policy which touched only the raw nerves of conscience and not the hard economic facts around which the political system revolves.[118]

The ins and outs of British negotiations with the

Community are outside the range of this study, but several highlights are useful in illuminating the confusing policies of the Labour Party. The story actually begins in 1949 when Jean Monnet and Sir Edwin Plowden of the Labour Government negotiated unsuccessfully for an economic union.[119] The Schuman Plan was announced only months later in May, 1950 and the sincerity of French interest in British membership is doubtful. Whatever the French view, the Labour Government was not interested, partly because of British nationalism and sovereignty, but also because the Plan was viewed as a romantic French solution to the "German problem." Ulrich Sahm concluded that:

> weakness, tradition-mindedness, and lack of vision on the part of her leadership caused Britain to lose what may prove to have been her last chance to assume leadership of Europe and thus to give history a new direction. [120]

The Common Market became an issue in 1960 under the Conservative Government of Harold Macmillan. The Prime Minister made an about face from previous Tory policy and announced that Britain "could not afford to stay outside the Common Market."[121] Labour, under the leadership of Hugh Gaitskell, declared outright opposition to what they regarded as a political maneuver. Of course, General de Gaulle solved the problem for both British parties by vetoing the United Kingdom's membership, an act which the NEC called "providential."[122]

The Macmillan negotiations forced Labour to develop a position on entry into the Community and the NEC did so on September 29, 1962, stipulating five broad conditions for Labour's support. These demands, still referred to in the 1975 referendum campaign, included:

(1) "Strong and binding safeguards for the trade and other interests of our friends and partners in the Commonwealth;"
(2) complete freedom in matters of foreign policy;
(3) fulfillment of the Government's pledge to the members of the European Free Trade Area (EFTA);
(4) the right to plan the British economy without interference;
(5) guarantees to safeguard the position of British agriculture.[123]

The Community became a major divisive issue within the party after the Labour Government of Harold Wilson applied for membership in 1970 shortly before the General Election. Though the Cabinet was somewhat split on the issue (Roy Jenkins and Barbara Castle were both Ministers) the middle ground was held by James Callaghan and the Prime Minister who "took a more pragmatic view

and judged the value of membership in terms of the particular bargain which the negotiators might achieve."[124]
The election manifesto of May 1970 reflected Wilson's
leadership in that it gave cautious support for the negotiations "provided that British and essential Commonwealth interests can be protected."[125] The party lost
the General Election and one year later, on July 7,
1971, the Government announced the entry terms and Labour attitudes catalyzed. In fact, while the 1970 Party
Conference retained a cautious support for entry, in
1971 the Conference declared oppostion to the terms by a
vote of 5,073,000 to 1,032,000.[126]

As the vote in Parliament on the treaty approached,
the PLP was divided into hostile camps. The Tribune
group of Labour MPs (the left wing of the Party) managed
to attract some moderates to their side while the "Labour Committee for Europe," which included about eighty
members of the PLP, supported entry.[127] The back-bench
revolt which the party suffered on October 28, 1971 when
the vote was taken is almost a classic in British politics. "In defiance of conference and whips, sixty-eight
MPs supported the government's motion approving the
principle of entry on the terms obtained, and twenty MPs
abstained."[128]

The renegotiations which led to the 1975 referendum
resulted from an NEC proposal of 1972 and were largely
"an attempt to heal the wounds" developed in 1970 and
1971.[129] Having won the 1973 general election, Wilson
proceeded with the negotiations which were completed in
1975. The special conference of the Labour Party held
on April 26, 1975 in order to debate the NEC position on
the renegotiated terms provides, through the transcripts
of speeches presented that day, a good account of the
currents of opinion regarding the Community which pre-
vailed in the party.[130] It seems that few wounds were
healed. The basic situation was that the Prime Minister
and his Foreign Secretary, James Callaghan, were locked
in combat with the NEC. The NEC's resolution won the
vote that day but "Her Majesty's Government" recommended
the opposite position to the British people and they pre-
vailed on election day.

The debate on April 26 was supposed to be about the
new membership terms, but it revolved largely around
questions of parliamentary sovereignty and the meaning of
socialist internationalism. Wilson, Callaghan, Roy Jenkins and John Mackintosh pleaded eloquently for a pro-
Market verdict, while Michael Foot, Bryan Stanley, and a
host of trade union representatives spoke for the NEC
position. Wilson warned against "narrow preoccupations"
in the midst of "the world war against man's primeval enemies of hunger and poverty, illiteracy, preventable dis-
ease and premature death." For him a decision to stay in
Europe was a constructive step in that war.[131] However,
the rejoinder was powerful: "As Socialists we should not

be concentrating on increasing the wealth and power of a section of Europe."[132]
The issue of whether pro- or anti-Market was the more socialist position pervaded almost every speech and generated more heat than light. When the question of sovereignty was raised the issues became concretized. Stanley started it off with a question: "Do we want to continue to be governed by those that we elect and can remove here in Britain or increasingly by a Commission in Brussels, backed up by a Community Court?"[133] Mackintosh meanwhile reminded the conference that "'Workers of the world unite' is not a slogan that stops at the channel."[134] A reading of the full transcript reveals that loss of parliamentary sovereignty was a key issue to the NEC, and decisions made in Brussels which affected food prices, for example, were of major concern to the trade unions.[135]
After the conference and the Government's success in the referendum the situation in Labour was "more of the same." Ron Hayward, the General Secretary of the Party during the European campaign, is a rabid anti-Marketeer.[136] The NEC produced a strong and negative background paper, The EEC and Britain: A Socialist Perspective in 1977,[137] and has continued opposition to any attempts toward further integration. In the meantime, Roy Jenkins became the President of the European Commission during this period and was an ardent supporter of the Community.
The issue of parliamentary sovereignty and consequent opposition to the expansion of powers of the European Parliament affected the NEC position on the direct elections. The Labour leadership began its analysis of the transfer of former national powers to the Commission in a manner similar to that of many pro-integrationists. That is, they pointed out that the Commission's regulatory power has reduced the sphere of policy decided upon by democratically elected legislatures. They further noted, and once again many pro-integrationists (particularly of the left) agree, that none of the national parliaments had sufficient control over decisions made by the Council of Ministers.[138] The NEC, however, found an anti-integrationist solution to the problem:

> The powers of the House of Commons to amend or repeal European legislation must be maintained if the rights of electors are to be preserved. It is in this context that any change in the nature of the European Assemby must be viewed. . . . If the Assembly did gain legislative powers, then the structure would be that of a federal state.[139]

Taking a historical view, the NEC recalled the growth of the House of Commons from a consultative to a legislative body and therefore concluded that:

> Those who believe that any change in the status of
> the EEC Assembly will grease the slope towards a
> federal or unitary state are pointing out the im-
> mediate need to strengthen the powers of the Com-
> mons over UK Ministers in the Brussels execu-
> tive.[140]

This determination to play down the role of the European Parliament led into a position firmly against the
direct elections:

> The fundamental argument against direct elections
> stems from an opposition to further integration and
> possible political union within the European Com-
> munity and a consequent belief that such inte-
> gration poses a threat to national sovereignty.[141]

Five specific objections to the principle of direct
elections, accepted by the NEC in 1978, led to a conclusion that the powers of the European Parliament would be
enhanced by direct elections in "transferring the right
of democratic scrutiny to a body less able than the UK
Parliament."[142] Other objections revolved around the
allotment of seats which protects small countries, the
large size of Euro-constituencies, and a denial of the
ability of the European political groups to work together effectively "in view of the very heterogeneous nature
of the political parties represented."[143]
As is obvious from the above, the Labour Party at
the official policy-making level is adamantly opposed to
any increase in the powers of the Community, even if
that increase cedes new rights to a democratically
elected Parliament. The root of this position seems to
be not socialism but nationalism. However, this attitude is not universal among party activists. One former
TUC official estimated that only ten percent of the
party was violently anti-Market and referred to this
group as "the xenophobic rump of the Labour Party."[144]
This same official conceded nevertheless that the anti-
Europe contingent holds power in the party, and he fore-
casted in October 1978 that Labourites who favored integration would face a tough battle with the NEC if they
proposed to run for seats in the European Parliament.[145]
The foregoing account of Labour's European activities makes the NEC position quite clear. What is much
more difficult to discern is the reasoning behind this
position. John Mackintosh thinks:

> "the anti-Europeans on the left see membership in
> the EEG as binding Britain into a community based
> on competition and on the expansion of those firms
> that can make a profit, so that the possibility of

creating a special Socialist economic system is gone forever.[146]

That is certainly an argument frequently advanced by the left, and any knowledge of the EC structure demonstrates that this evaluation of the Community is valid. However, when one begins to examine statements about the superiority of Westminster over European parliaments, thinly veiled attacks on the integrity of continetal socialist parties, and recalcitrant behavior in any attempts to formulate a unified European socialist position, a second conclusion seems warranted.[147] Though "xenophobia" may be too strong a term, the NEC and many anti-Marketeers seem to possess strong nationalistic and elitist attitudes. It is as if participation in the Community is soiling the world's oldest democracy. If one evaluates this undercurrent in conjunction with the lack of Marxist ideology in the party and the clear lack of efforts to work with other socialist parties, the rhetorically leftist agruments against the Community lose much of their punch. At times it seems that protecting the rights of British workers is far more important than advancing the position of European workers.

This conclusion casts considerable gloom over any predictions about the Labour Party playing a constructive role in the European Community. Divisiveness within the party and the negative attitude of the NEC seems to preclude the possibility of Labour working effectively within the Socialist Group for the kinds of European policies which could advance the economic goals of Labour's left wing. There is also reason to believe that a strong Labour delegation in the European Parliament would hinder efforts to transfer powers to that body. Even though there are pro-Europeans in Labour's ranks, the party's structure makes it doubtful that their voices will be heard.

CONCLUSION

The pivotal questions this study seeks to answer is how one creates a European structure which fosters pollitical integration. The preceding survey of the Community's three major socialist parties is pertinent to this task because it demonstrates some of the concrete difficulties which stand in the way of integrating the political parties of the Ten. Perhaps the overriding impression one develops through studying the SPD, PS, and Labour Party is the uniqueness of each of them.

There are commonalities among these parties, to be sure. Roots in the working class, commitment to social reform and governmental economic planning, strategies of evolutionary socialism - these exist within each party. Even in terms of the European Community, there is a common position that the institutions are in need of fundamental reform. Each of the parties also has a vocal left wing within which criticism of the Community_ is strident. However, these points of convergence cannot camouflage some striking differences. Contrasts begin with the historical milieu of each party's development. The longevity of the British constitutional system provided Labour with a stable atmosphere in which to develop as a parliamentary force, and to this day the Party leadership looks upon Westminster with pride and upon continental institutions with scorn. The French and Germans, it may be argued, have been sufficiently buffeted by changes in their political systems that they are less resistant to further change. The PS and SPD also share experience with coalition governments, a political arrangement of which Labour is highly suspicious.

The relative position of the left wing within each party is very important in regard to the Community and the direct elections. The Labour Left clearly dominates the NEC, and it was the NEC, not the Parliamentary Party led by James Callaghan, which dominated the direct election campaign. In France, the CERES faction of the PS is a force with which to be reckoned, but PS leadership is in the hands of the moderate and pragmatic Francois Mitterrand. Within the SPD the center and right hold the power. The Jusos can occasionally force programmatic debate, but they do not have the strength to control decisions.

Positions on the Community and its future development differ markedly. The SPD is solidly pro-Europe and frankly federalist. The PS is historically positive about the Community, but more cautious than the German Social Democrats. Labour, in clear contrast, is dominated by a National Executive Committee which is bitterly opposed to Britain's membership in the Community, and rabidly against further integration.

The following chapters will be concerned with the substantive debate and practical politics of the campaign for the first direct elections to the European Parliament. These chapters will discuss these three parties as they functioned in the context of the European campaign in 1978 and 1979. It seems probable after this examination of the SPD, PS, and Labour Party, that ideological divergence and national politics will be found to have great effects on the parties' participation in the campaign. It is possible that the explanatory value of these factors will be found to outweigh that of the neo-functionalist paradigm.

NOTES

1. See H. Kent Schellenger, Jr., The SPD in the

Bonn Republic: A Socialist Party Modernizes (The Hague: Martinus Nijhoff, 1968), pp. 10-18 for a discussion of the SPD's early years.
2. ibid., 12. Also see Vernon Lidtke, The Outlawed Party: Social Democracy in Germany, 1978-1890 (Princeton: Princeton University Press, 1966), pp. 320-326.
3. Schellenger, SPD in Bonn Republic, p. 12.
4. Joseph A. Berlau, The German Social Democratic Party, 1919-1921 (New York: Columbia University Press, 1949), p. 136.
5. Schellenger, SPD in Bonn Republic, pp. 19-21.
6. ibid., pp. 22-23.
7. Berlau, The German Social Democratic Party, p. 259.
8. Schellenger, "The German Social Democratic Party After World War II: The Conservation of Power," Western Political Quarterly 19 (June 1966): 260.
9. Stanley V. Vardys, "Germany's Postwar Socialism: Nationalism and Kurt Schumacher, " Review of Politics 27 (April 1965): 233.
10. ibid., p. 236.
11. Schellenger, "Conservation of Power," p. 254.
12. Framework of Economic and Political Orientation of the Social Democratic Party of Germany for the Years 1975-1985(OR '85), trans. Diet Simon (Bonn: Friedrich - Ebert - Foundation, 1976).
13. John H. Herz, "Social Democracy vs. Democratic Socialism: An Analysis of SPD Attempts to Develop a Party Doctrine," New York, The City College, pp. 11-18, provides background on the development of OR '85.
14. ibid., p. 14
15. OR '85, p. 8.
16. ibid., p. 11
17. William E. Lanx, "West German Political Parties and the 1972 Bundestag Election," Western Political Quarterly 26 (Sept. 1973): 514.
18. Paul Friedrich, "The SPD and the Politics of Europe: From Willy Brandt to Helmut Schmidt," Journal of Common Market Studies 13 (June 1975): 433.
19. ibid.
20. For discussion of the SPD's organizational structure see Gerard Braunthal, "The Political Function of the German Social Democratic Party," Comparative Politics 9 (Jan. 1977): 128-129.
21. ibid., p. 129. Herz provides a further discussion of the power struggle within the SPD in the early 1970s in his paper, "Social Democracy vs. Democratic Socialism."
22. Carlo Schmid, "Germany and Europe: The German Social Democratic Program," Foreign Affairs 30 (July 1952): 534.
23. Guy van Oudenhove, The Political Parties in the European Parliament (Netherlands: A.W. Sijthoff, 1965),

74

p. 48.

24. Geoffrey Pridham, Transnational Party Groups in the European Parliament," Journal of Common Market Studies 13 (March 1975): 266.

25. Ernst Haas, The Uniting of Europe (Stanford: Stanford University Press, 1968), pp. 138-139.

26. See for a discussion of these developments, Angela Stent Yergin, "West Germany's Sudpolitik: Social Democrates and Eurocommunism," Orbis 23 (Spring 1979): 51-72.

27. Willy Brandt, "Address to the European Parliament, Nov. 13, 1973, "Official Journal of the European Communities, Debates of the European Parliament, No. 168 (Nov. 1973), p. 21.

28. ibid., p. 22

29. Friedrich, "SPD and Politics of Europe," p. 433.

30. Texts Relating to the European Political Cooperation, 2nd ed. (Bonn: Press and Information Office of the Government of the Federal Republic of Germany, 1977).

31. This volume is available, free of charge, from the European Community of Information Office, 2100 M Street, NW, Washington, D.C. 20037.

32. European Political Cooperation, p. 161.

33. Vorstand der SPD, ed., SPD Dokumente zur Europapolitik (Bonn: Erich Ollenhauerhaus, Press and Information Office),p. 44. All translations from this document are by the author.

34. ibid.

35. ibid., p. 56

36. Yergin, "West Germany's Sudpolitik," p. 56

37. Europe Documents, No. 334, Aug. 6, 1965 (Brussels: Europe Agency for Press Information). Europe Press Releases are available at the Library of the U.N. Delegation of the Commission of the European Communities, 1 Dag Hammarskjold Plaza, New York, N.Y.

38. SPD, Europapolitik, p. 70.

39. ibid., pp. 70-74 discusses all facets of the SPD plan.

40. ibid., p. 70.

41. ibid, p. 72, and Europe, No 334.

42. SPD, Europapolitik, p. 74.

43. Maurice Duverger, "French Worries over Sovereignty: Europe for the Europeans," Manchester Guardian Weekly, Nov. 26, 1978. Duverger recounts the dispute between Schmidt and Giscard.

44. Brandt, "Address to the European Parliament," p. 25

45. SPD, Europapolitik, p. 5.

46. Brandt, "Address to the European Parliament," p. 24.

47. SPD, Europapolitik, p. 7

48. Baron Edward Castle explained in a personal interview at the House of Lords, London, Nov. 1, 1978,

that this is the opinion held by his wife, Barbara Castle, MEP, the leader of the Labour delegation to the directly elected European Parliament.

49. Europe, no. 334.
50. OR '85, p. 30.
51. ibid., p. 32.
52. William Paterson, "The SPD After Brandt's Fall: Change or Continuity?" Government and Opposition 10 (Spring 1975): 184.
53. See the discussion of this issue in Friedrich, "SPD and Politics of Europe," pp. 432-433.
54. ibid., p. 436.
55. Parti Socialiste, Socialist Manifesto for the European Elections (Luxembourg: Confederation of the Socialist Parties of the European Community, Nov. 1978), p.1.
56. For a detailed discussion of these two factions see Aaron Noland, The Founding of the French Socialist Party, 1893-1905 (New York: H. Fertig, 1970).
57. Byron Criddle, Socialists and European Integration: A Study of the French Socialist Party (New York: Humanities Press, 1969), pp. 10-12.
58. Noland, French Socialist Party, p. 49.
59. ibid., pp. 48-50.
60. Criddle, Socialists and Integration, p. 12.
61. ibid., pp. 12-13.
62. David S. Bell, "The Parti Socialiste in France," Journal of Common Market Studies 13 (June 1975): 419.
63. ibid.
64. ibid., p. 420. Also see Frank Wilson, The French Democratic Left, 1963-1969 (Stanford: Stanford University Press, 1971), chapter 5.
65. Sue Ellen Charlton, "European Unity and the Politics of the French Left, " Orbis 19 (Winter 1976): 1448-1450. Also see Bell, "Parti Socialiste," p. 420.
66. Charlton discusses these factions in "European Unity," pp. 1454-1457. See especially the chart on p. 1457.
67. Hans-Joachim Veen, The Position of Socialist and Communist Parties and the Integration of Western Europe (Bonn: Konrad Adenauer Stiftung, 1977), p. 17.
68. William Pfaff, "If Mitterrand Is Succeeded," International Herald Tribune, Nov. 17, 1978.
69. ibid.
70. ibid.
71. Private conversations with the author, London and Strasbourg, Nov. 1978. Since the PS took office in 1981, there is considerable evidence that this analysis is correct.
72. "Mitterrand s'explique sur la social-demo cratic," L'Express, Oct. 21, 1978, p. 112. Translation by the author.
73. ibid.

74. ibid., p. 117.
75. ibid., pp. 116-117.
76. Bell, "Parti Socialiste," p. 422.
77. ibid., pp. 425-426.
78. Veen, Integration of Western Europe, p. 14.
Also see "How to Lose an Election - Notes on the French Left," by George Ross, Brandeis University, April, 1978 (unpublished paper).
79. Veen, Integration of Western Europe, p. 14.
80. "Mitterrand s'explique," p. 114.
81. For a discussion of the SFIO and the ECSC see Criddle, Socialists and Integration, chapter 5.
82. ibid., pp. 46 & 49.
83. ibid., p. 49.
84. ibid., p. 80.
85. Europe Documents, No. 1614, Sept. 6, 1966.
86. European Parliament, Political Affairs Committee, ed., The Case for Elections to the European Parliament by Direct Universal Suffrage: Selected Documents (Luxembourg: Directorate-General for Parliamentary Documentation and Information, 1969), p. 336.
87. Mitterrand, "Un nouvel internationalisme," Le Monde Diplomatique, Feb. 1973. Author's translation.
88. ibid.
89. Michel Rocard, "French Socialism and Europe," Foreign Affairs 55 (April 1977): 558.
90. Parti Socialiste, Manifesto, p. 1.
91. Mitterrand, "Un nouvel internationalisme."
92. Rocard, "French Socialism," p. 557.
93. ibid. Also see Jane P. Sweeney, "Mitterrand's Economic Program: The Constraints of European Community Membership," paper presented at the Conference of Europeanists, Washington, D.C., May 1, 1982 for a discussion of conflicts between the Mitterrand government and the European institutions.
94. Edgar Pisani, MEP, interview, Palais de l'Europe, Strasbourg, France, Nov. 15, 1978.
95. Parti Socialiste, Manifesto, p. 20.
96. ibid.
97. Charlton, "European Unity," p. 1464.
98. ibid.
99. Paul Adelman, The Rise of the Labour Party, 1880-1945 (London: Longman Group Ltd., c. 1972), pp. 3-16 provides a good account of this phase of Labour's history. Adelman quotes Engels on P. 12.
100. David Marquand, "The Challenge to the Labour Party," Political Quarterly 46 (Oct. 1975): 396.
101. Bernard Crick, "The Future of the Labour Government," Political Quarterly 38 (Oct. 1967): 377.
102. Peter Jenkins, "Dilemmas of Social Democracy," Dissent 22 (Fall 1975): 346.
103. Jenkins, "The Future of the Labour Party," Political Quarterly 46 (Oct. 1975): 377.
104. Stanley Henig, European Political Parties: A

Handbook (New York: Praeger, c. 1969), pp. 405-406.
    105. Lord Wayland Kennet, former MEP, interview,
Palais de l'Europe, Strasbourg, France, Nov. 14, 1978.
    106. ibid.
    107. Crick, "Labour Government," pp. 378-379.
    108. Samuel Beer, British Politics in a Collectiv-
ist Age (New York: Random House, c. 1969), p. 140.
    109. ibid., p. 135.
    110. See Lidtke, The Outlawed Party and Noland,
French Socialist Party, in order to compare the early
years of the SPD and PS to those of Labour.
    111. Jenkins, "Dilemmas," pp. 346-347.
    112. Egon Wertheimer, "Portrait of the Labour
Party," in Richard Rose, ed., Studies in British Poli-
tics (New York: St. Martin's Press, 1966), p. 36.
    113. ibid., p. 38.
    114. Michael Foot, Speech before the Labour Party
Special Conference, April 26, 1975, in Labour and the
Common Market (London: The Labour Party, Transport
House, 1975) p. 41. This pamphlet contains the complete
transcript of the Common Market Conference.
    115. See National Executive Committee, Direct
Elections: Arguments For and Against (London: The Labour
Party, Transport House, 1976), especially item no. 5,
p. 4.
    116. Castle, Nov. 1, 1978.
    117. Jenkins, "Future of the Labour Party," p. 377.
    118. Peter Byrd, "The Labour Party and the European
Community, 1970-1975," Journal of Common Market Studies
13 (June 1975): 482.
    119. For a discussion of Labour and the Schuman
Plan see Ulrich Sahm, "Britain and Europe, 1950," Inter-
national Affairs (London) 43 (Jan. 1967): 12-23.
    120. ibid., p. 23.
    121. R.H.S. Crossman, "British Labour Looks at
Europe," Foreign Affairs 41 (July 1963): 733.
    122. ibid., p. 738.
    123. ibid., p. 739.
    124. Byrd, "The Labour Party," p. 471.
    125. Now Britain Is Strong: Let's Make It Great to
Live In (London: The Labour Party, Transport House, May
27, 1970).
    126. Michael A. Wheaton, "The Labour Party and
Europe, 1950-71," in Ghita Ionescu, ed., The New Politics of European Integration (London: Macmillan, c.
1972), p. 80.
    127. ibid.
    128. Byrd, "The Labour Party," p. 473.
    129. ibid., p. 474.
    130. Labour and the Common Market, available from
Transport House, is the best source for information on
this conference.
    131. ibid. pp. 7-8.
    132. ibid., p. 11 quotes Bryan Stanley.

133. ibid., p. 9.
134. ibid., p. 19.
135. ibid., p. 39 provides an example in Michael Foot's speech before the Conference.
136. Byrd, "The Labour Party," p. 474. Kennet also made it clear when interviewed that the NEC leadership is anti-Market. Also see David Butler and David Marquand, European Elections and British Politics (London: Longman Group Ltd., c. 1981), p. 65 for a discussion of the NEC's efforts to keep pro-Market MEPs from running in the 1979 campaign. Among those kept off the candidate list was Lord Kennet.
137. The Labour Party, The EEC and Britain: A Socialist Perspective (London: The Labour Party, Transport House, 1977).
138. ibid., pp. 62-64. Also see "The Anti-Tindemans Report," Agenor 57 (Dec. 1975): 13-21 for a discussion of left socialist positions on this issue.
139. Labour Party, The EEC and Britain, p. 65
140. ibid., p. 66.
141. NEC, Direct Elections.
142. ibid.
143. ibid.
144. Private conversation, London, Oct. 26, 1978.
145. ibid.
146. John Mackintosh, "The Problems of the Labour Party," Political Quarterly 43 (Jan. 1972): 13.
147. In addition to the transcript of the Labour Party Common Market Conference, cited above, consult the pamphlet against the 1975 referendum by the National Referendum Campaign, Why You Should Vote No (London: Her Majesty's Stationery Office, 1975).

3
The European Election Campaign: Structures and Issues

"L'Europe des Citoyens" is the evocative promise
of posters distributed by the European Community to
promote voter interest in the first direct election of
its Parliament.[1] This interest and the growth of a European ethos which could follow it are fundamental re-
quisites for the establishment of the "political community" Haas describes as the end product of integration.[2] Thus, a European election campaign has the
theoretical potential to create a significant alteration
of the status quo, that is, it might force the disequilibrium in the system which is an essential prerequisite
for the operation of the spillover dynamic.

This and the following chapter are focused on the
first direct election campaign. Their major question is
"What happened and why is it significant?" However, the
answer to this question is an intermediate step in this
study. "Why did it happen?" is the inquiry which will
provide the necessary link with Chapter One's critique
of neo-functionalism, and it will be the concern of the
final chapter. In order to conduct that evaluation, the
facts of the campaign must first be set forth. The process will be done in two parts: this chapter will investigate the European structures and major issues - the
skeleton of the campaign. Chapter Four will flesh these
out through an examination of the British, French, and
German national campaigns.

Structural arrangements to be studied include the
workings of the first direct elections as arranged by
the Nine, and the two organs of European socialist interaction - the Confederation of Socialist and Social
Democratic Parties of the European Community and the
Socialist Group of the European Parliament. An example
of how the socialists of the Community have worked together will be found in the third part of the chapter
which will examine the evolution of the joint election
manifesto of the Confederation's members. The fourth
section will compare the "Euro-issues" established by
the Confederation with the election manifestos of the

79

SPD, Labour Party, and Parti Socialiste.

PROCEDURES FOR THE DIRECT ELECTIONS

The Treaty of Rome established a European Assembly consisting of "representatives of the peoples of the states brought together in the Community," and further stipulated that "The Assembly shall consist of delegates who shall be designated by the respective Parliaments from among their members in accordance with the procedure laid down by each Member State."[3] The Treaty, while retaining the same procedures for selection of representatives employed by the ECSC, promised a significant change at some future time, and placed the responsibility for initiating this change within the Assembly:

> The Assembly shall draw up proposals for elections by direct universal suffrage in accordance with a uniform procedure in all Member States. The Council shall, acting unanimously, lay down the appropriate provisions, which it shall recommend to the Member States for adoption in accordance with their respective constitutional requirements.[4]

In 1960, shortly after the ratification of the Treaty of Rome, the Assembly submitted a draft proposal for European elections. However, the 1960s proved not to be a propitious time for expansion of democracy in the Community, and no serious steps toward direct elections were taken by the Council until 1974.[5] At that time during the Paris summit the heads of government made two structural decisions: to institutionalize their meetings and thereby create the European Council, and to go ahead with plans for the election of the Parliament by universal suffrage. Point twelve of their final communique reads:

> The Heads of Government note that the election of the European Assembly by universal suffrage, one of the objectives laid down in the Treaty, should be achieved as soon as possible. In this connection, they wait with interest the proposals of the European Assembly, on which they wish the Council to act in 1976. On this assumption, elections by direct universal suffrage could take place at any time in or after 1978.[6]

This agreement in principle began a process, by no means without problems and conflicts, which led to the elections on June 7 and 10, 1979. The first significant step in this process was the September 20, 1976 signing by the Council of Ministers of the "Act Concerning the Election of the representatives of the Assembly by di-

rect universal suffrage."[7] This Act, which established
the institutional framework for the elections, contains
one compromise provision which allowed it to be passed,
but also caused a one year delay in the timetable for
the first direct elections. Article seven of the Act
provides that "the Assembly shall draw up a proposal for
a uniform electoral procedure," however, it adds that
"Pending the entry into force of a uniform electoral
procedure... the electoral procedure shall be governed
in each Member State by its national provisions."[8] In
practical terms this article meant that each of the Nine
could and did use its chosen voting system in 1979. This
approach was largely necessitated by British recalcitrance about using a system of proportional representation.[9]

The Act having been signed, there remained two
rounds of voting in each national parliament before the
Council could fix a date for the election. Each parliament had to ratify the Act and then, because of the
stipulation of article seven, was free to draw up national electoral procedures. This process proved to be
too controversial and time-consuming for the elections
to take place in June 1978 as originally planned. As of
January 1978 the state of ratification and adoption of
election laws was uneven among the member states. All
but the United Kingdom had ratified the 1976 Act, but
only Denmark, Ireland, and France had completed the
adoption of electoral laws.[10] The House of Commons
finally approved its election bill in February 1978, but
because the district representation system chosen by the
British required the division of the electorate into
"Euro-constituencies" it was clear that the United Kingdom could not vote that spring.[11]

The Council of Ministers, meeting in Brussels in
March 1978, set the election dates for June 7-10,
1979.[12] The United Kingdom, France, and the Federal
Republic of Germany were each to elect eighty-one MEPs,
but by varying systems. The British insisted on single
member districts with their traditional "first past the
post" qualification for winning, the French chose
straight proportional representation with a single national list for each party, while the Germans elected
some seats nationally and some through the Länder,
though a proportional system was used.[13] Once these
hurdles were cleared the parties under study here knew
how and when they would compete in the first European
elections. It remained for them to decide the content
of their campaigns.

EUROPEAN SOCIALIST INSTITUTIONS

The socialist and social democratic parties of the
European Community come together in two organizations

whose membership and stated purpose differ substantially, though their ties are very real and of major importance. The Confederation of Socialist and Social Democratic Parties of the European Community, officially
headquartered in a small office in Brussels, is an organization of national party leaders and a regional af-
filiate of the Socialist International. The Socialist
Group of the European Parliament is composed of socialist and social democratic MEPs from twelve parties in
ten countries (since the Greek Pan-Hellenic Socialist
Union joined in 1981). It also has an extensive staff
drawn from the national parties. The several pages
which follow will describe the membership and structure
of both organizations, the type of issues with which
they deal, and the way in which national party members
interact in each of them. It should be remembered that
both were pivotal to an effective socialist election
campaign in Europe.

The Socialist Group

     From the outset, members of the Common Assembly of
the ECSC sat in transnational party groups, but they
spoke and acted as individuals for the Assembly's initial meetings. In January 1954 Guy Mollet and the socialists initiated a change in this procedure: Mr.
Mollet rose to the floor of the Assembly to state the
collective opinion of the Socialist Group.[14] Other
groups soon adopted this method, and by May 1954 when
the Assembly met to discuss the Second Annual Report of
the High Authority all of the groups (there were then
three) appointed spokespersons to expound their positions.[15] Thus, the socialists were leaders in strengthening the concept of transnational political groups.
Most studies of the histories of the groups accord to
the socialists not only historical leadership in group
development, but a high degree of coherence on issues
and cohesion in voting.[16]
     In discussing the Socialist Group as a possible
forum for integration several factors should be kept in
mind. The first is that the socialists and the Christian democrats both have excellent records for international cooperation, but that these records rest largely
on a period of Community history when little of controversy was decided by the Parliament.[17] Secondly, the
socialist parties of the Six had worked together in the
Common Assembly and then the Parliament since the early
1950s; a severe strain was placed on group cohesion with
the arrival of the British Labour delegation in 1975,
and then exacerbated in 1981 with the joining of the
Greek socialists (PASOK) who sit with the group but
retain the right to vote freely.[18] Lastly, an important
factor in the Parliament's composition is that most

persons of any party from any country who become MEPs have a strong interest in Europe. This factor has not been empirically documented, but indications point to a conclusion that individuals who make the personal and political sacrifices inherent in joining the ranks of MEPs have more in common with each other than do the broader memberships of party elites among the Ten.[19] This was particularly true before 1979, when all MEPs also served in their national parliaments.

The Socialist Group, in terms of membership and support organization at home, has been dominated by the SPD since the beginning. When Fitzmaurice did his study of the party groups in 1979 there were forty-seven socialists in the Parliament, seventeen of whom were German. The next largest national delegations were the French and the Italians with seven each.[20] After the arrival of the Labour Party and immediately before the direct elections there were sixty-three socialist MEPs: fifteen Germans, eighteen British, ten French, five Italians, the remainder a scattering from the smaller countries.[21] The Socialist Group in the elected Parliament has once again a preponderance of Germans, thirty-five among the 121 socialist MEPs. The Labour Party, whose results in the direct election were disastrous, now has seventeen members.[22]

Fitzmaurice found that with "small exceptions all the members come from Social Democratic parties, and all with the exception of the French party, in government or recently in government and with very similar traditions and concerns." For him these factors accounted for the group's basic cohesion.[23] These historical and political similarities have helped forge what Fitzmaurice called "a distinctly Social Democratic outlook."[24] The basis of this outlook is the socialist position on the market economy, the role of which the socialists seek to reduce whenever possible "and replace it by public provisions or intervention or, at the very least public control....At all times the burden of proof lies with the free enterprise system which is watched with scepticism by the Socialists."[25]

Geoffrey Pridham, in a study of the transnational groups undertaken in 1973, found the socialists to be the most united of the large groups. He attributed their unity to the disciplined nature of the national socialist parties, their approach to political issues which is "more doctrinaire" than that of the Christian democrats, and "a greater tradition of international fraternity, producing a similarity of outlook on most issues of integration."[26]

The coherence of outlook among continental parties represented in the Socialist Group, the preponderance of the SPD, and the group's internal camaraderie were all tested by the entry of the Labour Party in 1975. Despite the recalcitrance of the British (as discussed

in Chapter Two) the other socialists welcomed them
sincerely and set about forging the needed links with
the new MEPs.[27] The British, for their part, considered
themselves good parliamentarians and got down to work
with stereotypical forthrightness and fellowship. They
became active members of the Socialist Group, and there
is evidence that the experience of participating in the
Parliament lessened many misgivings about Europe - at
least among this small cadre.[28] Another factor which
deserves some consideration is that even though the
leader of the pre-election Labour delegation, John Prescott, was an anti-Marketeer, a good proportion of
Labour's first group of MEPs were sympathetic to European integration. Therefore, the Labour members of the
Socialist Group in the old Parliament tended to be more
cooperative with their European peers than was the
National Executive Committee (NEC).[29]

Provisions for staffing and financing political
groups and the patronage system which has developed in
the Parliament are factors which increase the power of
the political groups and strengthen ties with national
party activists. Each political group has a secretariat
with salaries paid from the Parliament's budget, but
appointment controlled by the group's leadership. In
this way, each group is assured of top level staff members with a political commitment to its goals. In the
Socialist Group the secretary general is appointed by
the group chairman, and he is then responsible for
hiring most of the remainder of the staff.[30] Funds are
allocated to the groups on the basis of the size of
their membership and certain other factors such as the
number of languages which must be translated in the
group's work.[31] Therefore, a large transnational group
like the socialists wields a considerable budget for
staff salaries, research, printing, translating, etc.
The chairman of the Socialist Group is thus a powerful
figure who can use patronage to build a staff loyal to
the goals espoused by the group. These staff appoint-
ments serve another level of usefulness as well: they
bring talented party workers to the Parliament for at
least a time, consequently building stronger ties with
the national parties.[32]

Several factors about the Socialist Group are
highly relevant to the direct elections campaign. The
first is their reputation for cohesion which caused
many analysts to expect the socialist parties to take
the forefront in waging a transnational campaign - an
analysis which may have been superficial, as we shall
see. Secondly, even within the group where relationships with British Labour MEPs in the late 1970s were
encouraging, the problem of integrating the Labour
members has been substantial.[33] Lastly, one strength
the socialists do have is a generous budget and a
committed and experienced staff in their secretariat.

The Confederation of Socialist Parties

On the Place de la Justice in Brussels the small storefront office of the Confederation of Socialist and Social Democratic Parties of the European Community functions as the center of European socialist cooperation. The Confederation office, quite a distance from the European Center, has the ambiance of crowded and cheerful confusion one associates with a temporary campaign headquarters. My own impression upon finding this office in October 1978 was that I was in the wrong place. This could not possibly be the center from which emanated the multi-lingual publications and the numerous activities of the Confederation. In time I came to discover that I was both right and wrong, and that the structure and role of the Confederation are complicated and important factors in all European socialist political activity, particularly the direct elections campaigns.[34]

The Confederation is the institutional link between the Socialist Group and the national parties which have members in the group. Technically, it is a regional grouping within the Socialist International.[35] Much more importantly, it is the Socialist Group's outreach organization, its channel for bringing the national parties together in order to further integrate themselves. As such, the Confederation is accorded considerable importance by committed Europeans who see it as a vehicle to further their goals, while it is treated with disdain by those who take an anti-integration stance. This is particularly true of the leadership of the British Labour Party.

The Confederation will be discussed here in terms of its structure and finances, its role in forming European socialist policies, and its links with the national party bureaucracies. Plans for the 1979 election campaign will be discussed in a later chapter.

According to the Socialist Group's press attaché, Jan Kurlemann, all of the transnational party organizations in the Community were organized by the Parliament's political groups in order to create the vital infrastructure for communication with the national parties.[36] Keeping that fact in mind, we need not be surprised that the Confederation's storefront office, described above, is only the tip of the organizational iceberg. The Confederation has very few paid staff members and minimal funds for publication, mailing, etc. Its only direct source of income is donations from the national parties which are naturally loath to contribute funds to a transnational organization which cannot help them to win elections at home. However, as do the other transnational party organizations in the Community, the Confederation receives both funds and staff support funneled through the Socialist Group. In practice, the

Confederation staff is almost entirely composed of employees of the Parliament whose official jobs are in the
Socialist Group's secretariat. Thus, the Socialist
Group's press office, for example, handles the Confederation's relations with the media. Translating and
printing are done through the group's budget. An illus-
tration of how this procedure works on a day-to-day
basis may be found through examining the group's monthly
newsletters published in the year before the direct
elections.[37] These publications, distributed free of
charge in all Community languages, are almost entirely
devoted to discussions of the Confederation's campaign
issues. Thus, the Community, in order to realize its
goals of furthering transnational political linkages,
pays the bill for a vast quantity of clearly political
communications.

The official members of the Confederation at the
time of the 1979 campaign were the national socialist
and social democratic parties from the Nine, as well as
the socialist parties of Spain and Portugal (the Greek
PASOK had not accepted invitations to join). The parties
are represented at Confederation conferences by their
national leaders, not their MEPs. At the Confederation's Tenth Congress in January 1979, at which the
European election manifesto was finally adopted, most of
the famous personalities of European socialism were
present: Mitterrand, Mauroy, Rocard, and Delors among
the French delegates; Bruno Friedrick, Ludwig Fellermaier, Erwin Lange for the SPD; Tony Benn, Barbara Castle, Ron Hayward, and Reg Underhill in the Labour delegation.[38] Of course, some of these names are also famous as rabid enemies of European integration. This is
particularly true of the NEC of the Labour Party which
makes it a practice to keep pro-Market party members
away from the Confederation.[39]

The nature of the Confederation is more than at
first meets the eye: it is staffed and supported by the
Socialist Group as their vehicle to further integration
among the member parties; however, the party leaders
with which it must work can easily be persons who oppose
its aims. My mention of this is not meant to indicate
that the Confederation is a useless organization. Quite
the contrary, it is an essential forum for the kind of
dialogue and debate which can eventually forge some common positions among the parties. The reality which
should be considered is that the socialist political
elites of the Community are not the prime movers for
transnational cooperation. They contribute little funding to the organization, they often send lesser officials with no decision-making power to Confederation
meetings, and they sometimes simply refuse to cooperate
with Confederation plans.[40]

In assessing the Confederation's role in the direct
elections campaign - which fell short of expectations -

we must regard its structure as a major factor. The existence of such an organization does not tell the whole story. Because it is staffed and supported by the "European" elite of the socialist parties, the Confederation's staff sees itself as a catalyst for integration. On the other hand, because the national parties only cooperate with Confederation plans when they choose to do so, any party can effectively thwart Community-wide action or pro-Europe infiltration among its own national electorate. The Confederation of Socialist Parties is a necessary creature of the Socialist Group, but it is weak because its energy emanates from the group, not the parties.

THE SOCIALIST APPEAL TO THE ELECTORATE

In a political situation in which the will of the majority prevails, a party platform or election manifesto is a good indication of where the majority of party activists stand on a host of issues. Also, because the majority has the power there is every political reason for the minority to cooperate, even if grudgingly. The Confederation of Socialist Parties is, however, an organization in which the enforcement of the will of the majority would fracture the tenuous ties which exist. Therefore, when the Confederation is able to produce a policy statement what occurs is a "least common denominator" situation: it must sift through the issues until it is able to find those on which everyone agrees. Minorities in such a situation have more power than their numerical strength indicates. The document which finally emerges has the strength of universal agreement. It may at the same time have the weakness of being equally unrepresentative of all because it says so little. The socialist parties of the Nine spent almost two years working and reworking a joint political statement for the first direct election campaign. The task proved a difficult one for several kinds of reasons - cultural, political, and ideological. As German MEP Erwin Lange explained in 1978, the British and Germans have totally different perspectives on how one writes a political manifesto. Stylistically, the British are terse while the Germans tend to thoroughly explicate every point. Mr. Lange observed that even if the SPD and Labour agreed absolutely on principles it would still be extremely difficult to agree upon a common text.[41] This kind of cultural problem is something which must be constantly dealt with by the transnational groups. Politically, the situations that the parties of the Confederation faced at home in 1979 were quite diverse. The French socialists, who perceived in the 1970s that a major national electoral victory for them probably required cooperation with the PCF, were reluctant to an-

tagonize the communists. The SPD, on the other hand,
because of the role communism has played in recent German history, cannot risk appearing sympathetic with parties further left than itself. Furthermore, at the time
the Germans led a government coalition with the Free
Democrats as their junior partners, a situation which
further limited the SPD's freedom of maneuver.[42] These
considerations have more to do with the practical business of winning elections than with ideological purity,
but they cannot be ignored by a party preparing to present its program to the voters. Different political
needs among the socialist parties were a very real tactical consideration as the joint election manifesto was
being discussed.

Differing ideological stances also played a crucial
role. The SPD does not use Marxist terminology since
1959 whereas the PS continues to do so. The Germans
are also pro-integration while the British leadership is
opposed and the French seem ambivalent at times. Even
if cultural and pragmatic political differences could
have been resolved by the Confederation, more fundamental disagreements would still have easily come to the
fore during the pre-election years.[43] The resolution of
ideological problems was made more difficult by the
postponement of the Labour Party's decision to participate in the Confederation until after the Common Market
referendum of 1975. By the time the British became active, the Confederation had already established working
parties to formulate proposals on external policy, economic policy, social policy, and Community institutions
for inclusion in the election manifesto.[44]

The obstacles facing those who favored a common socialist campaign having been discussed, we will turn to
the efforts to generate a political manifesto for the
direct elections campaign. The Confederation produced
two working documents and a final statement which was
actually distributed to voters in the spring of 1979.
A "Draft election manifesto of the Confederation of the
Socialist Parties of the European Community" was adopted
by the bureau of the Confederation on June 6, 1977. Discussion of this draft by the heads of the member parties
resulted in the "Political Declaration" adopted by the
party leaders in June 1978, and in a provision that
each party would be free to draw up its own election
manifesto for its national campaign.[45] Finally, in January 1979 at the Tenth Congress of the Confederation the
Appeal to the Electorate was approved.[46]

In examining these three documents it is possible
to distinguish the contrasts between positions thought
valid by the bureau of the Confederation and the working
parties, and those agreeable to all of the member parties. The first and most obvious difference is the
length of the documents, and consequently their specificity. The "Draft Manifesto" is twenty-seven pages in

length, the "Political Declaration" is eight pages, and
the finalized Appeal to the Electorate contains less
than five pages of text. These figures prove little in
themselves until they are correlated with the explication of issues in the successive documents.
The most obvious case of deletion of an issue concerns the socialist position on Community institutions
and further integration. The "Draft Manifesto" devotes
two pages to a discussion on "Democracy and Institutions." Positions stated here include several points of
criticism of current levels of democracy, and five sug-
gestions for structural and institutional changes. It
seems best to allow the writers to speak for themselves:

> There is therefore not enough democratic control
> over those areas which ceased to fall within the
> sphere of competence of the national parliaments
> when they became the responsibility of the Commu-
> nity.
>
> The transfer of responsibilities to the European
> Community and their extension ...must therefore be
> subject to the following conditions: that full dem-
> ocratic participation and control is guaranteed
> within the institutions of the Community, and that
> the powers lost by the national parliaments are
> transferred to the European Parliament;.... With
> regard to the responsibilities assigned to the
> European Community, Parliament is to exercise a
> legislative function, its decisions being submitted
> to the Council for approval.[47]

These general principles are followed by recommendations
for specific institutional modifications, among them
that "the Commission should be appointed by the Council
with the Parliament's assent," and that the Council
ought to immediately begin "to consider initiatives and
options of the European Parliament and to report to it
within a certain period on action taken."[48]
Turning to the "Political Declaration" of June 1978
one finds only brief references to the Community institutions, and these statements are distinctly different
in both content and spirit from the 1977 text approved
by the Confederation's bureau:

> The directly elected European Parliament must ini-
> tially develop within the framework of the existing
> treaties. We recognize that any further transfer
> of powers from national governments to the Commu-
> nity institutions or from national Parliaments to
> the European Parliament can take place only with
> the clear and direct assent of the national govern-
> ments and parliaments.[49]

The 1978 text does include other references to a "democratic Europe" and "democracy and socialism" as the "guarantee of peace and freedom."[50] However, it nowhere defends the idea of increasing the powers of the Parliament or of strengthening the central institutions in any way. The same text on Community institutions, quoted above, which the party leaders agreed to in June 1978, is retained in the Appeal to the Electorate. There is no further mention of adding to the structures of political integration. One principle stated in the Appeal, "To bring economic and social development under democratic control," appears at first glance to be concerned with this subject, but it actually discusses "cooperation between countries" and worker control in local industrial planning.[51]

Any student of the Socialist Group can quickly assess what happened to the issue of political integration. The original draft, composed by the "Europeans" of the Confederation's bureau, was unacceptable to the national party elites, or, to be more exact, to a few of them. The procedure of including only those principles unanimously agreed upon required the deletion of strong and positive statements about strengthening the institutions. What remains in the document is a testimony to national parliamentary sovereignty.

Another interesting area of revision - although it is more rhetorical than substantive - occurred in the introductory statements of the three documents. These passages, which attempt to describe European socialism, changed dramatically in content and emphasis through subsequent revisions. The "Draft Manifesto" of 1977 devoted several pages to an introduction. A few of the major points include the following:

> We intend to bring about a change in the economic and social structures of our countries. But each of those countries today is too small to do so alone; only European integration can succeed in doing this.

> Our Socialist parties have inherited a different experience down the years. They operate in countries where the level of economic development, intensity of social struggle, cultural traditions, awareness of social problems and the interplay of internal political alliances profoundly differ.[52]

By 1978 there were several textual changes and some softening of the European thrust of the "Draft Manifesto"; but the thrust was still toward Europe. The statement quoted above, "Our parties have inherited different experiences..." remained in the 1978 document.[53] Several other statements were dropped, but their replacements

could not be considered outrightly offensive to integrationists. "Our drawing more closely together in Europe
is quite compatible with respect for each other's indi-
viduality." Liberating "the individual from every form
of dependence" and enhancing the "power and rights" of
each person are the socialists' June 1978 goals. To
achieve them "we must change the economic and social
structures of our countries. We realize that whilst
each country can by itself do much toward this end,
joint action between us in some fields can accelerate
our progress."[54] This introduction is briefer and not
as blatantly pro-Europe as the 1977 document. However,
it still retains support for integration while acknowl-
edging national differences. European socialism is consistently presented as a heritage all of the parties
share with a set of goals they all intend to further.
The 1979 Appeal to the Electorate makes a much
weaker presentation of these themes. The 1977 statement
that "only European integration can succeed" in changing
economic and social structures is gone. Instead, all
one finds is that the members of the Confederation
"share a common goal of a new world order based on Socialist principles."[55] In fact, the word "integration"
does not appear at all in this version of the introduction. As close as the document comes is a statement
that "actions undertaken in common could, in various
fields, accelerate the progress toward these goals."[56]
The one section of the original draft which remains intact is the one which begins "Our parties have inherited
different experiences."[57] Even in regard to this statement, its change in position in the document seems to
strengthen its importance. In the 1977 and 1978 versions it was an early thought which was in a way rebut-
ted by what followed. In 1979 it became the closing
paragraph. Thus, the reader is left with a sense of
differences rather than of commonalities. Political
rhetoric is not always important in itself. It matters
here, I think, because it provides an example of what
the national leaderships of the Confederation's constituent parties view as common to all of them. It is not
very much.
     In all three documents an explication of necessary
changes in economic and social policies forms the core
of the socialist argument. Except for the change in
emphasis from strengthening the center to calling for
greater cooperation between countries and national parliaments, the issues themselves change little. The 1977
"Draft Manifesto", for example, spells out in detail an
eight point plan for changing economic and social policy. The points include full employment, income distribution, economic democracy, improved benefits, living,[58]
and working conditions, and educational opportunities.
The Appeal's social and economic issues include the
right to work, democratic control of economic develop-

92

ment, an end to discrimination, "particularly against
women," and the defense of human rights and civil liber-
ties.[59] Reading both documents, it seems fair to conclude that the Appeal is calling for the same kind of
social democratic reforms as the earlier document, but
doing so with no explication of specifics. There is no
real change in direction.

The foreign policy of the Community - both political and economic - is a secondary but important consideration for the socialists. The "Draft Manifesto" discusses "External Policy" in three major areas: relations
with the superpowers, a common Community foreign policy
(European Political Cooperation), and relations in general. Major emphases are on Europe as a "third force"
between the United States and the Soviet Union, and on
developmental assistance to the third world. The parallel section of the 1979 Appeal, entitled "Promoting
peace, security, and cooperation," differs with the
first document in several respects. The most notable
difference is the absence of any discussion of the
United States. In 1977 the bureau agreed that, while
they did not see confrontation with the United States
as necessary for establishing a European identity, cooperation on an equal basis was an important goal. This
was particularly true, they argued, because democratic
socialism was more advanced in Europe than in the United
States.[60] By 1979 discussion of European relations with
the superpowers was compressed into a single sentence:
"Socialists in Europe will therefore contribute to the
pursuit of détente between East and West."[61] Absent
also were any specific references to European integration as a method of furthering socialist goals in the
international arena. In 1977 the direct elections were
lauded as a means of strengthening the international
prestige of the Parliament and the Community as a whole.
No such expectation was stated in 1979.

Discussion of aid to the third world changed in a
more subtle manner. The first text emphasized a number
of specific steps to be implemented by the Community.[62]
The most important are still included in the Appeal, and
a concern about more generous and equitable aid programs
is evident. However, whereas the original document
seemed to indicate that the Community should coordinate
aid programs, my interpretation of the text of the
Appeal is that the socialists should encourage the member governments to take these steps at the national
level.[63]

The document presented to the European electorate
by the Confederation of Socialist Parties had the inherent strength of being acceptable to all of the member
parties. However, it also had the weakness of being so
vague that each member party had to adopt its own program in order to capture the votes of its national electorate. This situation is reminiscent of the cliché

about whether a glass is half empty or half full. The
Socialist Group's press attaché, Jan Kurleman, was enthusiastic about the level of success: the Appeal to the
Electorate was used by every Confederation member in its
national campaign. Even the Labour Party distributed
it.[64] However, the version of the Appeal used in Britian contains a statement by Ron Hayward:

> This Declaration agreed at the Brussels Congress of
> the Confederation of Socialist Parties of the Euro-
> pean Community is not a statement of party policy
> but is issued for information as an indication of
> our general approach. The Labour Party Manifesto
> for the Direct Elections, published in January,
> 1979, sets out the policies on which the British
> Labour Party will be fighting the campaign this
> summer.[65]

One must pause and ask whether a national party - particularly a European socialist party - would enter an
important election campaign allowing each local party
grouping to write its own election manifesto. It would
seem that the party leaders in the Confederation - at
least in their dealings in regard to the European election - have not achieved a European consciousness nor
even a sense of any political need to take a common position on substantive issues. The preparation of the
final version of the Appeal to the Electorate may be
viewed as a typical example of reaching compromise positions in a transnational organization which makes decisions only on the basis of unanimous consent.
   The process of whittling down the "Draft Manifesto"
until the final Appeal was agreed upon in January 1979
raises the question of the spillover dynamic which is
essential to neo-functionalism, that is, one can ask
whether coming together to discuss the manifesto resulted in increased levels of cooperation and compromise. This question makes relevant the examples of positions adopted by the bureau of the Confederation and
rejected or considerably altered by the national party
leaders. Classic socialist positions like a demand for
full employment and calls for disarmament remained because they are universally accepted in social democratic
circles. They are also issues about which the Parliament can do little more at present than act as a European pressure group. The issue which became most difficult and which was virtually sidestepped in the final
document was the future evolution of the Community itself. In short, the problem of trying to unify the
campaign in all of the nine countries reveals two levels
of difficulty: the socialists failed to come up with a
viable transnational program, and the central issue they
failed to address adequately was European integration
itself. These are reasons for these problems, and some

of them have great pragmatic validity.[66] Nevertheless, there does not exist in the present Community a counter-weight to any pragmatic reasons for a lack of cooperation. More important for the future, even the socialist parties do not seem ready to lead the way to a democratic government for Europe.

THE NATIONAL PARTY MANIFESTOS

If the Appeal to the Electorate is presumed to be the statement of what the Confederation members agree upon about the Community, the other side of the story may be found in the national party manifestos.[67] The section of this chapter which follows will investigate the European election manifestos of the Labour Party, Parti Socialiste, and SPD. Particular attention will be given to party statements about issues not concretely treated in the Confederation's Appeal. This method will highlight differences among the parties, so it should be reiterated here that the three parties tend to agree on broad social and economic goals. The best arena of change - national or European - and the specific content of broad goals are the disputed issues. Because the three manifestos differ in style, length, organization, and content, they cannot be immediately discussed through a comparison of parallel thoughts. They will first be summarized individually, then contrasts and comparisons will be addressed.

The SPD's Election Manifesto

The German Social Democratic Party prepared an exhaustively detailed manifesto for the European elections. It seems, however, that the content of the document raises the same kinds of issues as do the manifestos of the other parties. A brief glance at the manifesto quickly reveals its basic approach: pro-integrationist and humanistic. A more thorough investigation of its contents should allow for a forthcoming comparison on substantive policies with the French and British socialists. For this purpose, in choosing SPD positions to be discussed here an attempt will be made to concentrate on those issues which the other parties also address. Introductory remarks, employment and industrial democracy, agricultural policy, foreign relations, and European institutions seem the most crucial for the sake of comparison.

It comes as no surprise that the SPD begins this statement with dramatic praise of the Community: "The principle of Social Democracy, the undeniable unity of humanity and social justice, is to cross the frontiers of national states under such political order."[68] The

SPD identifies four principles of democratic socialism, "peace, humanity, democracy and solidarity," and two evils in Europe, "Capitalism and Nationalism."[69] Because the SPD was committed to choosing representatives to the League of Nations by universal suffrage, they can validly call the first direct election to the European Parliament "an overdue historic step."[70] There is a tenor of transnational ethos in these opening pages: references to the other members of the Confederation, mention of great socialists of the past who were not Germans, gratitude for the end of nationalistic wars in Europe. A pro-integration and cooperative stance is taken up immediately.[71]

Full employment - one goal on which these three parties agree - is explained as a condition whose attainment will "only be successful after some time as the problems involved are, to a considerable extent, of a structural nature."[72] The subsequent discussion of means to this end addresses itself to the Community-wide dimensions of the problem, and goes so far as to recommend that "any financial policy adopted by weaker member countries to deal consistently with the employment problems should be supported from Community funds."[73] Many specifics, such as special attention to youth, coordination of national policies, and increasing service sector jobs are common to the position of the French PS. In order to achieve social justice through policies such as these, the SPD advocates the participation of workers and their representatives in industrial planning, both in the public and private sectors.[74]

The German position on regional policy is worth mentioning as a measure of integrationist sincerity simply because the Federal Republic has the highest standard of living among the Ten and hence the least to gain from regional projects. On paper at least, the SPD calls for a regional policy which contributes toward levelling out the differences in the living standards of the various regions of the Community. This includes raising living standards by creating new opportunities for the development of "handicapped regions" and increasing the budgets of the EC Regional and Social Funds.[75] One might argue that on this one issue the SPD and the Labour Party agree. Yet, Labour's self-interest in regional policy (as will be discussed) cannot be denied, and their demand that the Community spend more in the United Kingdom does not lend credence to a pro-integration interpretation of their position.

The SPD recognizes agriculture as the area in which "the integration within the European Community is farthest advanced."[76] Nevertheless, they find criticism of the Common Agricultural Policy (CAP) justified and join in demanding urgent reform. Their problems with the CAP as it has developed are three: it benefits big farmers in favorable regions; it penalizes consumers; and it is not properly "interrelated with the problems of the world's food supply."[77] These shortcomings of the present policy should be addressed, according to the SPD, in correlation with long term plans for regional, industrial, and labor market policies. This way, as they reason, the Community budget will have to provide an increased amount for policies which address socio-economic structural problems to the detriment of agricultural price supports.[78]

Relations with the United States were not touched upon in the Labour manifesto, while the PS presented a biting attack on the U.S. The SPD takes a more moderate line than the French socialists, couching its criticisms of American attempts to dominate Europe in delicate language. For example:

> The federation of the nine European states will provide a chance of being an even stronger partner to North America.... Europe will not try to find a new identity through confrontation with the USA but through cooperation as their equal partners.[79]

The German position is clear enough, though it is hardly an aggressive, socialist stance toward American capitalism.

Observing the political groups in the directly elected European Parliament, it became apparent to the SPD that a search for the Parliament's identity was underway, and the issue of its rights and powers vis-à-vis the Council must eventually be joined.[80] In this evolving confrontation the SPD sees as crucial party group positions regarding the institutions. The SPD - the Socialist Group's numerically dominant party - takes an approach to institutional development which can only be called federalist. They "are demanding that this direct election should be associated with more rights for the European Assembly."[81] Among those rights are review of legal acts of the Community and of Commission policy, the right to pass legislation, and the power to appoint members of the Commission on nomination by the Council and to pass a vote of censure on them.[82] At the same time they want the Council to make majority decisions as provided for in the Treaty. All of this, they hope, will speedily lead to a European federation with a democratic constitution to "provide an adequate political framework for a self-determination of the European peoples and citizens."[83] These positions can only evoke potent opposition from the Labour Party, while they are also far more radical than anything to which the PS would agree at present.

The SPD is probably the least "socialist" of the Confederation's members.[84] It is also the most integrationist of the large parties. The party's strength in the Socialist Group was most likely a major reason be-

hind the pro-integration thrust of the 1977 draft of
the Confederation's manifesto. Nevertheless, by 1979
only the SPD among the major Socialist Group members
continued to espouse hopes and plans for immediate federation of the Nine.

The French Socialist Manifesto

The leadership of the Parti Socialiste is not
pleased with the present European Community. However,
whereas the British socialists present a nationalist
anti-integration critique, the French present a socialist pro-integration critique. In other words, the PS
wants reform, but it does not want this reform to weaken
the Community. One notes this emphasis in the introduction to the French election manifesto. The direct
election is hailed as "an event of great importance
which will have a lasting impact on the future of our
nation and the everyday life of the French people."[85]
The Community is described as an organization "based on
technocratic know-how rather than popular support," but
this situation is not viewed as a reason to abandon it:

> Since, however, capitalist exploitation is increas-
> ingly organized on an international scale, and
> since in the face of this threat the solidarity of
> those affected is beginning to take on an inter-
> national dimension, the Socialist Party considers
> that the fight it is conducting in our country must
> inevitably be extended to Europe.[86]

The upbeat attitude of these introductory remarks continues throughout the manifesto. The document devotes
about one-third of its twenty-four pages to a discussion
of why socialists must be Europeans and why the liberal
approach has failed in Europe. There then follows a set
of specific policies to which the PS commits itself.
Europe is presented as a "decisive continent" because of its position in both East-West and North-South
relations. The United States is criticized with zest
for economic policies which "are designed to weaken
Europe, first and foremost."[87] In this situation, with
the United States fighting to maintain its control, "the
policy of France cannot be a return to a new isolation."[88] Because the policies of recent French governments have led, according to the PS, to "uncontrollable
laissez-faire" in the midst of crisis, and to the pen-
etration of France by multinational corporations, France
cannot afford to break Community ties: "This could only
result in massive economic and social decline from which
the workers would be the first to suffer."[89] In contrast with Labour and the SPD who make no head-on attack
on capitalism or on the United States, the French per-

ceive regional problems which require a regional solution. The Community is taken to task for the structure of the "Common Market" itself. Non-tariff barriers which still exist are noted, and the conclusion that "American multinational corporations are the main beneficiaries of the system as it actually emerged" is criticized.[90] In the midst of discussing these economic shortcomings of the Community, one large political success is noted: "permanent reconciliation with Germany."[91]

Skepticism about all of the common policies is included in the PS critique of the European status quo. The Social Policy is described as a "grandiose title" which "barely conceals a humble reality."[92] The low level of funding for regional development is equally decried. The fault of capitalism in all of this is clearly addressed:

> The crisis which has prevailed since 1973 ... has revealed the plain truth that the free play of this brand of liberalism has clearly not brought about a reduction of social and economic inequalities.[93]

The solution to all of this, as the PS sees it, is to elaborate a French socialist strategy which can change policies both in France and in Europe. It is acknowledged that within the Community at present "The national centers of power retain ultimate responsibility." However, while the PS saw in 1979 the urgency of "the attainment of national power," the leadership also believed "the achievement of its program by a Government of the Left in our country would encounter substantially less opposition if our European environment were less influenced by liberalism and Atlantic interests."[94] With this situation and its own future in France in mind, the PS set forth a series of measures which it pledged to support in the directly elected Parliament. Issue areas include employment, social, regional, industrial, and agricultural policies, control of multinationals, monetary policy, integrated planning, enlargement, relations with the third world, and Community institutions. For each of thirteen areas the manifesto first delineates the current situation and then makes concrete recommendations for change. A few examples of these policies should be sufficient to provide a sense of the direction in which the PS would steer the Community.

Employment policy is the first issue raised, and the discussion revolves around the European dimension of the problem, not just the situation in France. The suggested changes are what one might expect from socialists who are also integrationists. The PS wants to step up industrial activity in the Community, utilizing democratic planning methods and making full employment the primary goal, rather than one of the "mere by-products of growth." They also advocate the creation of new jobs in sectors which would aid the disadvantaged both by providing the jobs and by improving available services (education and health, for example). An end to discrimination, a thirty-five hour work week, and vocational training facilities where they are most needed are additional recommendations. Always, the solutions to unemployment are aimed to assist all European workers.[95]

The PS admits that the CAP "has been generally beneficial to our country in the past," but still calls for its radical revision, especially with the prospect of further enlargement of the EC.[96] The kind of change the French propose is more creative than the simple elimination of price supports. They want "the reorientation of Community expenditures towards the improvement of farm structures, greater social welfare and restoration of regional equilibrium." Special attention to Mediterranean products and coordination with third world producers are also advocated.[97] Once again, there is no allusion to specifically French needs (but, obviously, concern about Mediterranean agriculture has an element of self-interest) and there is a propensity to expand central coordination while diverting its goal from the needs of the market to the needs of workers.

The PS position on the development of Community institutions is of major intetest in this particular study, so it will be the final issue area explored here. The argument has three facets. First, the PS wants, "within the context of the existing Treaties, better democratic control of Community life, and greater participation by the working world in the decision-making process." This is to be done through the European Parliament which should monitor "all those measures which at present elude direct scrutiny by the national Parliaments."[98] Secondly, the extension of the Community's powers is not advocated as an immediate step, but should be delayed until "the EEC has adopted the aims set out in this Manifesto."[99] The third facet of the PS position consists of three specific proposals: more input from the Parliament in Community decision-making, representation of workers on the various planning committees within the European bureaucracy, and "possible adjustment of the Community's powers and resources in the context of the procedures laid down in the Treaties" if this becomes necessary to implement the PS's proposals.[100] The French do not want a capitalist Community so powerful that it can make socialism in the member countries an unattainable goal. However, they are willing to trust the European Parliament to watch over the Council and Commission in the present, and to eventually strengthen the Community if it proves capable of encouraging socialist solutions to Europe's problems. This

approach sees integration as a means - not an end - but
certainly as a viable channel for achieving a socialist
Europe.
The Parti Socialiste's European election manifesto
can thus be viewed as an ambitious and positive program.
While addressing blunt criticism to the Community as it
existed in 1979, the French PS developed a series of
proposals to advance socialist goals in all the member
states. Far more cautious about immediate federalism
than their West German counterparts, the leaders of the
PS nevertheless enunciated a series of proposals which
would, over time, dramatically increase the power and
areas of competency of the European Parliament.

The British Labour Party Manifesto

Labour adopted its European election manifesto on
January 24, 1979, not quite two weeks after the Confederation approved the Appeal to the Electorate. The manifesto is terse, blunt, and reflective of the thinking
of the anti-Marketeers who hold sway on the NEC. The
opening lines are indicative of the mood of the entire
document:

> In this Manifesto, we set out Labour's policies for
> the fundamental reform of the EEC. This is not a
> programme of government - for the European Assembly
> does not have and must not have, the right to over-
> ride our own Parliament and decide government
> policy.[101]

Labour's two major themes, reform of Community institutions and the sanctity of Westminister, are thus clear
from the outset and are the constant subjects of all
that follows.
The specific issue areas addressed in the document
include "The Role of the Assembly," democratic control
of the economy, the Community budget, agriculture, fish-
ing, energy, and relations with the third world. The
Assembly, the budget, and agricultural policies are the
most crucial concerns of Labour, as will be demonstrated.
Whereas the other parties which were discussed
tended for the purposes of the electoral campaign to
dramatize the importance of the Parliament, the NEC saw
fit to encourage British voters to elect candidates to
the Parliament who would prevent its future development.
Voters are reminded that the EC Assembly (Labour never
calls it the European Parliament) "is not a real Parliament...it is largely a consultative body. We believe it
should remain so."[102] The fact to which pro-integrationists point with pride, that decisions of the European Court and Commission regulations are binding in the

member countries, is viewed with considerable alarm because it is presently accompanied by a lessening of the powers of the House of Commons. The other socialist parties agree on the whole with this criticism, but the Labour Party's solution is unique. The leadership is flatly opposed to granting new powers to the Parliament because Labour is not "prepared to see the EEC develop into a new federal 'superstate'."103

Rather than remedy the lack of democracy through further political integration, Labour supports an amendment of the 1972 European Communities Act "so as to restore to the House of Commons the power to decide whether or not any European Economic Community regulation, directive or decision should be applicable to the United Kingdom."104 Labour would like the Treaty of Rome amended along these lines, but "failure to gain Community approval for this fundamental change will not deter us in any way from passing the necessary legislation at Westminster."105 Remembering the changing position on European institutions in the Confederation's several versions of the European election manifesto, it becomes clear why all they could finally say on the subject was that the national parliaments would háve to approve the transfer of any additional powers to Europe.106

Labour's discussion of democratic control of the economy also takes a nationalistic bent. When the Confederation discussed democratic control in the Appeal they concentrated on worker participation in industrial decision-making and control of multinationals.107 The British socialists mean by this term that economic decisions ought to be made on the national level: "We believe that the long-term solution lies in the British Government having the freedom to apply Labour's industrial policies."108 Though there is mention of a desire to "work with our socialist and trade union partners," this is for the purpose of reaching economic goals within each member state.109

Discussion of the budget, which Labour believes is unfair to the United Kingdom, follows almost identical lines to those of the argument presented by Mrs. Thatcher to the Council in December 1979.110 The British of both parties find the budget intrinsically unfair to them because of the preponderance of agricultural price supports in the Community's expenditures. However, Labour not only wants the CAP reformed; they also demand "a sharp reduction over the years, in real terms, of the absolute size of the budget itself."111 The British parties may be correct in their analysis of how the Community spends its money, and British politicians are certainly not alone in calling for changes in agricultural policy. What is perhaps most important here is Labour's desire to reduce the total amount of money which flows through the Community's administration. Agricultural policy per se is first considered in

terms of its effect on consumers. "We do not believe
that European consumers ...should subsidize backward
agriculture through inflated food prices."[112] Discussion on restrictions on such imports as New Zealand lamb
and butter, Australian beef, and Canadian wheat recalls
the comment of one continental socialist that the British have always paid deflated prices for food because of
preferential arrangements within the Commonwealth.[113]
Whatever the case, Labour wants to see "national governments taking an increasing responsibility" for agricultural price supports.[114]
     Fishing and energy are discussed very briefly. The
Common Fisheries Policy "cobbled together shortly before
British entry" is summarily condemned. No new policy is
detailed. The only energy issue mentioned is retention
of British control over North Sea oil:

> We are entirely opposed to the transfer of any pow-
> er to control energy or energy policy from member
> states to the Commission, the Council of Ministers,
> or the Court. We will insure that the benefits of
> this country's indigenous fuels are retained for
> the British people.[115]

     Community policy toward the developing world is
treated along lines very close to the Confederation's
position. Labour calls for socialist economic and trade
policies as the only solution to poverty and underdevel-
opment.[116] There is no call for an increase in Community coordination of aid policies, but there is an in-
sistence on some changes in developmental policy. Specifically, India should receive more Community aid. The
CAP also comes under attack for subsidizing some products and consequently glutting the world market.[117]
     Giscard d'Estaing observed in 1979 that "it re-
mained to be seen whether Britain could learn proper
'Community behavior'."[118] He was concerned at the time
about the conduct of Mrs. Thatcher and her Conservative
government, but as one reads Labour's European election
manifesto a question can easily occur: Do the British
want to destroy the Community? The Labour authors
seemed to look for and emphasize the shortcomings of the
Community. The overriding policy Labour set for itself
in the campaign was to roll back European integration.
Socialism does not seem to be the root of this attitude.
A peevish nationalism is more evident, and its effect on
the Socialist Group's campaign will be discussed later.

Reflections on the Manifestos

     Reading the Appeal to the Electorate in isolation
one can easily presume incorrectly that it is a summary
of major positions of the Confederation's members. If

one instead reads it along with the 1977 draft approved
by the Confederation's bureau and the manifestos of the
individual parties, a very different picture emerges.
The Socialist Group, particularly the pre-Labour Socialist Group, has a superb record for cohesion on issues
within the Parliament.[119] The group, however, is not
the Confederation, nor do its members necessarily represent mainstream positions within their parties. Another
reality is that the Parliament seldom if ever has anything to decide upon which is both controversial and important. The Parliament has most often acted as one
concerted pressure group against the prerogatives of
Council and Commission.[120]
    Let us suppose for a moment that the European Par-
liament now had the power to legislate. The Socialist
Group could not hope to act upon substantive legislation
based on a common mandate emerging from the positions
taken in the Appeal to the Electorate. Two thoughts result from considering such a situation. First, if the
power to legislate were granted tomorrow, it is conceiv-
able that the unity of the Socialist Group would shatter
in a matter of hours. There is another side to that
possibility, however. What if the power to legislate
had existed before the direct elections? Would that
have, through sheer necessity, given the national parties the impetus to hammer out a concrete European electoral program? To state the question as it was raised
in the Introduction to this study: if there existed democratically controllable power at the Community's center
would the parties make the compromises necessary to
grasp it? The existence of the Appeal may be viewed as
a proof of the success of the neo-functionalist method;
the emptiness of the document may point out neo-functionalism's great weakness.
    For the researcher whose main purpose is to explore
the theoretical and practical dimensions of European socialism, these campaign materials provide a rich source
of insights. However, their contributions to this study
are of a different order. Here, the existence of substantive and unresolved differences is important not because of ideological content per se, but because this
demonstrates that the major socialist parties simply
do not agree on the European Community itself or its
policies. Who is the better socialist or the better
European is not the pivotal question which arises.
Rather, one needs to ask about the parties' level of motivation to integrate themselves. It is possible that
integrative goals and behavior are not caused by the
spillover dynamic espoused by the neo-functionalists,
but by political considerations whose causes fall outside the explanatory capability of the neo-functionalist
paradigm. This possibility will be discussed after the
national campaigns and their results are investigated in
Chapter Four.

CONCLUSION

The purpose of this chapter has been to set out the structures and issues which formed the basis of the socialist campaign for the first directly elected European Parliament. Several of the observations made on earlier pages will be summarized here for the sake of clarity. The election's "rules of the game" are, strangely enough, not terribly important to this study's eventual conclusion, yet they are necessary for understanding the campaign. Also, the difficulties encountered in achieving a unanimously approved electoral plan at the level of the Council of Ministers, and further problems encountered in securing the necessary legislation in the parliaments of the Nine add some insight to our understanding of the obstacles to be overcome in furthering political integration in Europe.

The fact that the Confederation of Socialist Parties is an infrastructure created out of the needs of the Socialist Group - and largely funded by the Group - is another consideration to be remembered when one has the urge to point to its existence as a sign of integrative sentiment on the part of its member parties. The difference between Socialist Group and Confederation staff attitudes, on the one hand, and those of national party elites on the other, can be great. Furthermore, the consensus method of decision-making within the Confederation can result in what may be called "no risk" integration. The national parties have to give very little, both financially and ideologically. They, and not the Confederation, are still the dominant reality.

My observations on the various campaign manifestos were considered above. All that needs to be reinforced here is that the hopes of the Confederation's bureau that the socialists would mount a unified campaign were not realized. The reasons for this disappointing outcome will be delved into at a later time.

It may seem to readers, and correctly so, that in the preceeding discussion emphasis was placed upon the problems encountered in efforts to integrate Europe's socialist parties. The reason for this critical approach was to establish the fact that surface indications of cooperation were only a small part of the European campaign. By glossing over the substantive areas of disagreement among the member parties of the Socialist Confederation one may be able to validate the presumptions of the neo-functionalist paradigm. The disadvantage of such an approach is that it cannot unearth possible shortcomings in the "Community method," and hence cannot discover any better means for achieving transnational political integration in Europe.

105

NOTES

1. This and other European campaign posters may be
obtained from the European Community Information Office,
Rue de la Loi 244, Brussels, Belgium.
2. See the discussion of political community in
Chapter One, pp. 9-10.
3. A Parliament for Europe (Luxembourg: Secretariat
of the European Parliament, June 1978), pp. 6-7.
4. ibid., p. 6. The Treaty of Paris establishing
the ECSC contained the same provision as Article 138 of
the Treaty of Rome, cited here.
5. Élections directes: Un Parlement de 410 Sieges
(Paris: European Parliament Information Office, July
1978), p. 6. Also see European Elections, a press packet
available from the French Embassy to the United Nations,
New York, distributed in May 1979.
6. European Elections: A Parliament for the Community (Luxembourg: Secretariat of the European Parliament, Oct. 1977), p. 9.
7. ibid., p. 13. This booklet contains the complete
text of the Act.
8. ibid., p. 15.
9. One British MEP told me in a private conversation in London, Oct. 1978, that proportional representation was "responsible for Hitler."
10. "European Report," Jan. 12, 1978, File 423.02,
Library of the Delegation to the United Nations of the
Commission of the European Communities, New York, NY.
11. "European Report," Feb. 17, 1978.
12. "European Report," March 7, 1978.
13. French Embassy, European Elections, details the
voting procedure used within each of the nine countries.
14. Guy van Oudenhove, The Political Parties in the
European Parliament (Netherlands: A.W. Sijthoff, 1965),
p. 48.
15. ibid.
16. Perhaps the most thorough study of the political
groups is John Fitzmaurice, The Party Groups in the
European Parliament (Lexington, Mass.: Saxon House, Lexington Books, c. 1975). Also see Geoffrey Pridham,
"Transnational Party Groups in the European Parliament,"
Journal of Common Market Studies 13 (March 1975): 266-
279.
17. For a discussion of political issues in parliamentary debates see Stanley Henig, European Political
Parties: A Handbook (New York: Praeger, 1969), pp. 474-
495.
18. Private conversations with socialist MEPs,
Palais de l'Europe, Strasbourg, France, Nov. 14-17,
1978.
19. The sacrifices are substantial. MEPs spend at
least two weeks of every month in Brussels attending
committee meetings, and in Luxembourg or Strasbourg at

106

parliamentary sessions. This allows little time to develop one's national political career.
20. Fitzmaurice, Party Groups, p. 87.
21. European Socialist (Brussels, June 1978), p. 12. This monthly magazine is an official publication of the Socialist Group of the European Parliament.
22. The importance of the Labour delegation's role, which exceeds its numerical strength, will be discussed in a later chapter.
23. Fitzmaurice, Party Groups, p. 87.
24. ibid., p. 95.
25. ibid., p. 96.
26. Pridham, "Transnational Party Groups," p. 271.
27. Efforts to integrate the Labour delegation were discussed with Erwin Lange, MEP (SPD) and Edgar Pisani, MEP (PS) on Nov. 15. 1978, Palais de l'Europe, Strasbourg, France.
28. Both before and after the direct elections I attended Socialist Group caucuses in Strasbourg. Under the terms of my presence there, the proceedings I observed cannot be publicly discussed. It does seem appropriate to note that antagonistic viewpoints notwithstanding, group members work together with candor, humor, and pragmatism, and they do so in six languages.
29. Lord Wayland Kennet, interview, Palais de l'Europe, Strasbourg, France, Nov. 14, 1978.
30. Fitzmaurice, Party Groups, p. 87.
31. Pridham, "Transnational Party Groups," p. 269.
32. ibid., p. 275.
33. This conclusion is based on several private conversations with Socialist Group MEPs, Nov. 1978 and Oct. 1979.
34. Most of my understanding of the Confederation stems from the following interviews: Michael Wood, Secretary, Labour Delegation to the European Parliament, London, Oct. 31, 1978; Ben Paterson, European Parliament Information Office, London, Nov. 2, 1978; Jan Kurleman, Socialist Group Press Attaché, Strasbourg, Oct. 24, 1979.
35. "European Socialists on the Eve of the Direct Elections," (Luxembourg: Confederation of the Socialist Parties of the European Community, June 1978), p. 6.
36. Kurleman, Nov. 15, 1978.
37. The newsletter, European Socialist, is available from European Parliament, Socialist Group, 3, Bd. de l'Empereur, 1000 Brussels, Belgium.
38. For a complete listing of the participants see European Socialist, No. 3 (1979), pp. 27-28.
39. Kennet, Nov. 14, 1978.
40. About one particularly important, but frustrating meeting, a private source said, "People didn't come so we couldn't vote." This person says that the failure of top national leaders to attend meetings is a major problem for the Confederation.

41. Lange, Nov. 15, 1978.
42. "L'Eurosocialisme, un myth," Le Republicain Lorraine, June 26, 1978. The same problem was mentioned by Helga Köhnen, Palais de l'Europe, Strasbourg, Oct. 24, 1979.
43. "Conseil de Famille," Le Monde, June 26, 1978.
44. "European Socialists on the Eve," p. 10.
45. "Conseil de Famille."
46. "Draft Election Manifesto of the Confederation of the Socialist Parties of the European Community," June 1977; "Political Declaration," June 1978; and Appeal to the Electorate, Jan. 1979. All are available from the Confederation of Socialist Parties, European Center, Luxembourg.
47. "Draft Manifesto," p. 4.
48. ibid., p. 5.
49. "Political Declaration," p. 7.
50. ibid., pp. 7-8.
51. Appeal to the Electorate.
52. "Draft Manifesto," pp. 1 & 3.
53. ibid., p. 1, and "Political Declaration," p. 1.
54. "Political Declaration," p. 1.
55. Appeal to the Electorate.
56. ibid.
57. "Draft Manifesto," p. 1, "Political Declaration," p. 1, Appeal.
58. "Draft Manifesto," p. 6.
59. Appeal.
60. "Draft Manifesto." p. 21.
61. Appeal.
62. "Draft Manifesto," pp. 25-27.
63. Appeal.
64. Jan Kurleman, Oct. 24, 1979.
65. Ron Hayward, "Foreward," Appeal to All EEC Electors (London: Labour Party, Transport House, 1979), p. 1.
66. Practical difficulties can be very serious for the parties. They include coalition governments at home, differing levels of friendship with the U.S., and upcoming national electoral issues.
67. English versions of the election manifestos of the SPD, PS, and Labour Party were obtained from the Confederation of Socialist Parties, 22 Place de la Justice, Brussels, Belgium.
68. SPD, "Programme of the Social Democratic Party of Germany for the first direct elections of the European Parliament," (Brussels: Confederation of Socialist Parties, April, 1979), p. 1.
69. ibid., pp. 2-3.
70. ibid., p. 5.
71. Helga Köhnen explained on Oct. 24, 1979 that the SPD wanted to contest the election based on one substantive European Socialist Manifesto.
72. SPD, "Programme," p. 9.

73. ibid., p. 11.
74. ibid., p. 24.
75. ibid., pp. 34-35.
76. ibid., p. 42.
77. ibid., p. 43.
78. ibid., pp. 44-45.
79. ibid., pp. 73-74.
80. This growing sense of the Parliament's power was evident at the Plenary Session of Oct. 24, 1979 when Foreign Minister O'Kennedy of Ireland presented the annual report of the Council of Ministers on European Political Cooperation, and responded to questions. Parliamentarians were vocal about their belief that the Council does not adequately consult them.
81. SPD, "Programme," p. 62.
82. ibid., p. 63.
83. ibid., p. 65.
84. Paterson, Köhnen, and other persons interviewed seemed to agree that the SPD is to the right of the other members of the Socialist Group.
85. Parti Socialiste, "Socialist Manifesto of the French Socialist Party for the European Elections," Oct. 21, 1978 (Brussels: Confederation of Socialist Parties, Nov. 1978), p. 1.
86. ibid.
87. ibid., p. 3.
88. ibid.
89. ibid.
90. ibid., p. 5.
91. ibid., p. 4.
92. ibid., p. 5.
93. ibid., p. 6.
94. ibid., p. 7.
95. ibid., pp. 9-10.
96. ibid., p. 11.
97. ibid., p. 12.
98. ibid., p. 20.
99. ibid.
100. ibid.
101. Labour Party, "Manifesto of the British Labour Party for the European Assembly Elections," Jan. 24, 1979 (Brussels: Confederation of Socialist Parties, April, 1979), p. 1.
102. ibid., p. 2.
103. ibid.
104. ibid., p. 3.
105. ibid.
106. Appeal to the Electorate.
107. ibid.
108. Labour Party, "Manifesto," p. 3.
109. ibid., p. 4.
110. "Thatcher Raises the Market's Roof," New York Times, sec. 4, Dec. 2, 1979.
111. Labour Party, "Manifesto," p. 6.

112. ibid.
113. Private conversation, Palais de l'Europe, Strasbourg.
114. Labour Party, "Manifesto," p. 7.
115. ibid., p. 8.
116. ibid.
117. ibid.
118. "Thatcher Raises the Market's Roof."
119. Fitzmaurice, Party Groups, pp. 87-93.
120. Henig, European Political Parties, pp. 474-495.

4
The European Campaigns
of Three Socialist Parties

Actions, according to the familiar cliché, speak
louder than words. The last chapter of this study was
concerned with words: the various political manifestos
in which the European socialists presented their positions to voters in the campaign for the first direct
elections to the European Parliament. It was found that
the individual manifestos of the Community's leading socialist parties differed markedly in issues raised and
in their general thrust. Furthermore, it was demonstrated that these differences coupled with the structure of the Confederation of Socialist Parties served
to produce a European Appeal to the Electorate which was
very weak in terms of specificity of content. Yet,
analysis of issues and ideological positions provides
insight into only one aspect of the direct elections
campaign. It is possible that the actual shape taken
by the campaign was more positive in terms of political
integration than the parties' political statements would
have led one to expect. Therefore, this chapter under-
takes an exploration of the pragmatic aspects of the
campaign, with the aim of completing the description of
what happened in this historic European event.

In order to examine the national campaigns of the
Labour Party, SPD, and Parti Socialiste, it is necessary
to place them in the broader context of European pre-
electoral activity in general. This area of essential
background will be treated in the first section of this
chapter. Then the study will turn to an examination of
campaign plans and activities of the Confederation of
Socialist Parties of the European Community. After discussing the socialist campaign from a European perspective, the third part of the chapter will investigate the
national campaigns of the three parties. In concluding
this chapter I will attempt to assess whether national
politics or European socialism was the primary reference
point for each party. It will also be necessary to make
some assessments about differences and similarities in
the three campaigns, and about the place of transnation-

al socialist efforts in each party's electoral activities.

THE EURO-CAMPAIGN: GENERAL OBSERVATIONS

The success of any political party's election campaign is most often and most easily assessed by examining the results of the polling. Even in this study, which is more interested in the conduct of the socialist campaigns than in the number of newly elected MEPs from the Confederation's constituent parties, the election results are important information. The national outcomes, the post-electoral strength of the transnational political groups, and figures on voter turnout in the nine countries which participated add to the available evidence about the campaigns of Labour, the SPD, and the PS. Thus, we begin this discussion with the end of the Euro-campaign.

Results among the four largest countries (Britain, France, West Germany, and Italy) are most important because among them they controlled 324 of the 410 seats in the 1979 European Parliament. Though their populations differ in size, they were each apportioned eighty-one seats. Results for the major parties in each country are as follows:

France: UDF, 25; Gaullists, 15; Socialists, 22; Communists, 19; Britain: Labour, 17; Conservatives, 60; Italy: Christian Democrats, 30; Communists, 24; Socialists, 9; West Germany: SPD, 35; Christian Democrats, 42; Free Democrats, 4.[1]

The outcome in the major countries formed the core of the transnational groups' strength, though socialists and Christian democrats picked up a considerable number of seats in Belgium and the Netherlands. European totals made the Socialist Group the largest with 111 members, but with the European People's Party (Christian democrats) claiming 107 seats and possessing potential allies in the Conservative and Liberal Groups, socialist hopes to dominate the assembly were dashed.[2]

The Christian Democratic and Socialist Groups remained the most transnational, with socialists elected from all nine countries and Christian democrats from six. Communists won forty-four seats, forty-three of them in Italy and France. Conservatives in the new Parliament totaled sixty-three, with sixty elected from the United Kingdom (UK).

Voter turnout is another relevant set of data. Across the Community, slightly over fifty percent of the eligible voters participated, and while this is good by American standards it is lackluster for Europe. The rate of participation differed markedly among the Nine. In

Belgium and Luxembourg, where voting is mandatory, ninety percent of the electorate turned out. Italy, only
one week after a general election, had an eighty-five
percent participation rate, in stark contrast to the UK
where about thirty-three percent of the eligible voted.[3]
The sixty percent turnout in the Federal Republic was
far below the eighty-five to ninety percent average in
post-war West Germany. It is also interesting to note
that in West Germany the turnout was lowest in traditional SPD strongholds. As one SPD activist observed,
"The workers are not interested in Europe."[4]
    Commentaries on the meaning of all these numbers
abounded in the European and American press. Political
observers seemed to agree on several conclusions. Chief
among them is that the center and center-right parties
exhibited the greatest strength, a result which followed
the trend in national elections in the late 1970s. An
editorial in Le Matin provides perhaps the best summary
of the results:

> One lesson is clear from the results of the Euro-
> pean election: the conservative and centrist par-
> ties obtained the best scores in all the countries.
> 'Europe will be Socialist or it will not be,' de-
> clared Francois Mitterrand. The reality is oppo-
> site: Europe will be indifferent and bored, and it
> will be centrist, that is to say bourgeois and
> materialist.[5]

    The second almost-universal observation is that
pro-Community parties fared far better than those who
opposed the Community in their campaigns. The British
Labour Party and the French Gaullists (RPR), both of
whom waged anti-Community campaigns, are the illustra-
tive cases here. Labour won seventeen of eighty-one
seats, and the RPR claimed only fifteen of France's
places in the Parliament. The results were political
embarrassments to both parties. In Britain it was Labour's second disgrace within a few weeks, and in France
the Gaullist showing was considered a significant defeat
as the parties jockeyed into position for the 1981 presidential election.[6] The only other major party which
opposed the Community was the French Communist Party
which won nineteen seats, less than their socialist
rivals and less than Italy's communists. It would seem
on the basis of this evidence that an anti-Community
position did not go hand in hand with electoral success.
Perhaps this is because persons supportive of integration were more likely to vote.
    The role of the British Labour Party evoked wide-
spread comment on another level: they were viewed as
the spoilers of the Socialist Group's chance to dominate
the directly elected Parliament. If one considers the
left totals in the major countries, Labour's debacle

becomes clear. Socialists and communists attained thirty-three seats in Italy, thirty-five in West Germany,
and forty-one in France. Against those figures, Labour's seventeen seats are an obviously poor result. Socialists on the continent hoped that Labour would bring
a bloc into the Parliament comparable to the thirty-five
member SPD contingent. As James Goldsborough noted:

> Although the European Socialist Group will be the
> largest, it falls far short of a majority in the
> 410-seat body. Much of the blame for this was put
> on the British Labourites, whose lackluster per-
> formance in the election cost the European Social-
> ist Group heavily.[7]

Another newspaper account concluded, "The main reason
for the Socialist parties' lost ground was the collapse
of the British Labour Party vote in the European election."[8]
    The actual campaign can be described in terms of
the activity of the elites and the response of the
masses. Political leaders, whether because they were
interested in Europe or because they simply turned on
their usual campaigning routines, threw themselves into
the campaign. They received substantial support in
their efforts from the Community institutions, as will
be discussed. Another sector of the elite, political
commentators and political scientists, also swung into
action with a resultant glut of newspaper columns and
special features about the significance of the direct
elections.[9] However, if public response can be accu-
rately gauged by the percentage of persons voting, in
most countries it was far below the national norm. The
biggest reason for this, according to the commentators,
was that people did not understand the issues.[10] (The
Italian turnout belies this simplistic analysis. The
average turnout for the original Six was seventy-one
percent. In Italy the turnout was eighty-five percent,
one week after a major national election.)[11]
    The Community leadership was well aware long before
the election that voter apathy could result from a lack
of information about the Community and the Parliament.
Therefore, the Commission allocated substantial funds
for general informational advertising.[12] In all,
twenty-six million dollars were spent on non-partisan
advertising, with fifteen million dollars devoted to
providing information about the Parliament and the Community, seven hundred thousand dollars used to assist
national broadcasters with public information programs
about the direct elections, and over ten million dollars
allocated for a "get out the vote" effort. Most of this
work was not done directly by the Community, but was
contracted out to private advertising firms.
    Informational materials were prepared for distribu-

tion during the ten-month period before the election. Most widely used was a pamphlet called The European Parliament which explains the history and function of the body, the role of political groups, and the mechanics of the direct elections.[13] Its style is suitable for students, labor union members, and the average literate voter. This publication was distributed throughout the Community in all languages.

The "get out the vote" effort was organized, contrary to original plans, on a country-by-country basis. The national approach was thought to be the most effective way of dealing with differing voter conceptions of the Community among the nine electorates. In countries where voters and parties were favorable to the Community - Germany, Italy, Ireland, Belgium, Luxembourg, and the Netherlands - the campaign was aimed at arousing voter enthusiasm. In France, where positions on the Community differed greatly among the major parties, care was taken to concentrate on themes about which the parties agreed. In Britain and Denmark, where opposition to membership is substantial, the thrust was toward a directly elected European Parliament as a means of citizen control. Thus, Belgian posters proclaimed the advent of "Europe of the Citizens," while in France, where many voters do not want to be citizens of Europe, the theme was "Choisissez votre Europe"("Choose your Europe").[14]

Commission studies of the results of its publicity drive showed positive results. A survey conducted one month before the election indicated that eighty to ninety percent of the potential voters were aware that the direct elections were taking place. Also, the Commission found that the press was covering the event extensively and that demand for informational publications was "massive."[15]

In the midst of these carefully orchestrated efforts, the European public responded with some ambivalence. Surveys conducted through the Commission's "Euro-Barometer," an extensive semi-annual poll, point to general awareness and acceptance of the election, but little enthusiasm. The January 1978 Euro-Barometer found seventy-two percent of Europeans in favor of the direct election, but only fifty percent concluding that the election was "an event with important consequences which is certain to make Europe more politically unified."[16] Also, only one out of two persons interviewed declared an intention to vote. Survey results in May 1979 did not differ substantially.[17] Seven out of ten interviewees still thought the elections to be a good thing. It was also calculated on the basis of this questionnaire that about sixty percent of the eligible voters would turn out. This was close to accurate, but assessments about individual countries were wrong in several cases.[18]

Public attitudes and voter turnout seem to have been affected by the interplay of three factors: the importance of success to party "regulars", public sense that something of importance was at stake, and voter confusion about what was happening. In France, it may be argued, the first two factors were at play. The proportional direct election was seen by the major parties as a test of strength for the forthcoming presidential election.[19] Thus, party activists saw a definite need for broad participation, and consequently worked for high turnouts. Also, in France there was a debate on substantive issues. Voters of the right and of the left had clear choices between pro- and anti-Community parties. In the Federal Republic it can be demonstrated that all parties took a pro-Community stance, and according to one SPD activist the low working class turnout resulted from a sense that the Community was far away and of little importance in people's everyday lives.[20] In Great Britain, the Labour Party was thoroughly demoralized by the general election which put Thatcher's Tories in power. That factor made the European election somewhat anti-climactic. Added to that, Labour sent mixed signals to the voters. Their message was essentially "Send us to Europe so we can stop Europe from happening." The Conservatives, buoyed by national success and clear on their European positions, swept the election.

One overriding observation about the campaign is that Community-wide issues were of little interest to the voters. It seems that wherever the contest was fierce or interesting, it was because of a local issue or some national political implication.[21] One well-placed person in the Socialist Group believes that the campaign was a non-event because it came "either too early or too late." This person believes direct elections would have evoked great enthusiasm in the 1950s, or, that opportunity missed, after the Parliament had been granted substantive powers. However, the contemporary malaise about Europe and the relative unimportance of the European Parliament served to undercut the integrative potential of the campaign, according to this source.[22]

This brief discussion of several aspects of the first direct elections campaign warrants several conclusions. The first is that the campaign and electoral results differed greatly from country to country. Secondly, patterns of participation and victory/defeat cannot be detected on a Europe-wide left-right continuum: the left won over fifty percent of the seats in France, close to fifty percent in Italy and West Germany, and about twenty percent in the United Kingdom. Thirdly, in pragmatic matters, the media campaign for example, the "Europeans" who made the original plans had to capitulate to differing national realities rather than treat-

ing Europe as an organic unit. Although results of the
polling reinforced national trends during the 1970s, and
although elites took an energetic role, the publics were
cool, particularly in the UK and surprisingly in West
Germany.

THE SOCIALIST CONFEDERATION'S TRANSNATIONAL CAMPAIGN

The title of this section is a misnomer. The Confederation of Socialist Parties of the European Community did not wage a transnational campaign, and in fact
its members made little effort to do so. However, the
bureau of the Confederation, with the aid of funds sup-
plied by the Socialist Group, organized some activities
designed to serve three purposes: to create rapport
among the socialist candidates, to provide the European
media with evidence of socialist unity, and to build a
transnational element into the individual national campaigns. These activities, their successes and failures,
and the levels of cooperation with them exhibited by the
Confederation's member parties are the subject of the
next several pages. Throughout this discussion, the
structure and limitations of the Confederation, as discussed in Chapter Three, should be borne in mind.
The staff of the Socialist Group and the Confederation undertook four types of activities during the campaign: the design and use of common visual symbols, publication of materials for distribution to the voters,
organization of special conferences for the candidates,
and acting as a clearing house for speakers and information. The success of each project can be evaluated in
terms of press coverage as well as the extent to which
national parties availed themselves of the aid offered.
The common emblem designed by Otl Aicher and
adopted at the June 1978 meeting of party leaders in
Brussels was perhaps the most transnational feature of
the socialist campaign. The basic symbol, a blunt white
arrow on a red field, was designed for use alone or with
other arrows in the colors of the national flags.[23] Although, as the French communist newspaper, l'Humanité,
remarked drolly, the arrow pointed to the right,[24] the
use of the traditional socialist colors, the simplicity
of the design, and the incorporation of the national
flags appealed to all of the member parties. In examining campaign materials distributed by the national parties it is striking to note that this symbol was almost
exclusively used. Samples of West German, French, British, and Italian campaign literature and posters are all
alike in only one feature: this red and white arrow
motif.[25] It is not surprising that the SPD used it because Otl Aicher is a popular German graphic artist and
SPD member.[26] However, in November 1978, Walter Brown,

Labour's Assistant National Agent, stated that Labour
had no intention of "confusing the rank and file voters"
with any European emblems.[27] Labour's apparent change
of heart on this matter was their only significant cooperative gesture during the campaign.
The widespread use of the common emblem may or may
not be important. Perhaps its major implication is that
the voters learned to identify their parties through new
symbolism. No study has been done to ascertain whether
the voters realized the emblem stood for the unified
efforts of all the Confederation parties. Therefore,
attitudinal change at the mass level cannot be verified,
but elite efforts to identify their parties with the
Confederation are clear. It is concurrently true that
in some cases symbolic identification was as far as national leaders were willing to go, but there seems to
have been a sense that some link with the Socialist
Group was advantageous to the success of the campaigns.
The common use of the socialist emblem can also be contrasted with the media campaign of the Commission in
which different graphics were used with each national
electorate.[28]
The monthly newsletters of the Socialist Group were
all devoted to the Confederation's campaign issues during the six months preceeding the June 1979 elections.[29]
Similar publications are financed for all political
groups by the Parliament as a means of building the
strength of their transnational party organizations.
Newsletters of the Socialist Group are published in all
Community languages, but have a uniform content. European Socialist is mailed directly to all persons on the
group's mailing list, and is also available at all Community and Parliament information offices. The publication is usually twelve pages in length, but several expanded issues were produced during the campaign.
The contents of several issues of this newsletter
can serve as an example of the socialist information
campaign. The February 1979 issue is titled, "European
Elections: A New Opportunity for Women?"[30] It contains
brief articles about the Parliament's role in shaping
social policy regarding women, and about the Confederation's position and Socialist Group's efforts concerning
women's rights, family life, care of the elderly, con-
sumer protection, and peace - issues presumed to be the
concern of women. While the relevant passages from the
Appeal to the Electorate are cited, they are expanded
upon substantially. The March issue is a report on the
Tenth Congress of the Confederation in January 1979.[31]
Photographs of Europe's better known socialists are set
amidst reprints of major speeches delivered at the Congress. The speeches chosen for publication discuss employment, the economic rights of citizens, and Europe's
role in securing world peace - issues of agreement among
the member parties. In April European Socialist was

ɪsed to report on the specialized conferences conducted
.n member countries by the Confederation during the pre-
ᴇlection year.[32] Other 1978-1979 issues covered such
:opics as employment, regional policy, and enlargement
ɔf the Community.[33]

Examining the various newsletters one can find a
ɔasic "line" which is consistently espoused: socialists
ɪave a distinct world view, and working together in the
ᴂarliament can further it. The publication's primary
ᶠunction seems to be the strengthening of ties between
.he Socialist Group and ordinary voters. It is impos-
ɜible to assess the impact on individuals, but one ad-
ᵛantage is that European Socialist does not have to pass
:hrough the hands of any obstructionist national leaders
ɪn its way to readers. Group control rather than Con-
ᶠederation control insures that. However, a monthly
ɪewsletter from a distant organization cannot be com-
ɔared in impact with personal contact with candidates
ᴇspousing certain issues.

Realizing this political fact, and also understand-
.ng that many Euro-candidates were unschooled in Euro-
ɔean issues and even the day-to-day working of the Par-
.iament, the staff of the Socialist Group-Confederation
ᴂroposed a series of conferences in the individual coun-
:ries and a meeting of Confederation candidates in Lux-
ᴇmbourg. These conferences had the potential of fur-
.hering the Confederation's three aims in the campaign:
ᵍaining local media coverage, educating candidates, and
ɔringing the European dimension of the campaign closer
:o the voters.

The basic plans for a series of conferences had
ɔeen set by October 1978.[34] The idea was to have a con-
ᶠerence on a particular theme in each of the nine coun-
:ries. The Socialist Group would pay the bills while
:he national party played host. Speakers would include
ᴇuropean socialists with an expertise in the issue at
ᴴand, and candidates from other countries would be in-
ᵛited, along with important national figures. Thus, the
:onferences would assist the national parties' campaigns
ᴡhile projecting the transnational image of the Social-
.st Group. The key to the plan was the willingness of
ᴇach national party to host such an event.

Conferences were scheduled and occurred in every
:ountry but the United Kingdom. The British Labour Par-
.y maintained, until it was too late, that Labour needed
ᴴo assistance from the Socialist Group.[35] Descriptions
ɔf a few of the conferences are representative of the
ɔthers. The first, on employment, was held on December
.4-15, 1978 in Amsterdam. The major speaker was the
ᶠormer Dutch prime minister, Joop den Uyl, and he was
ᵍoined by Jacques Attali(PS) and Helmut Minta(SPD).[36]
ɪndustrial democracy was the subject of the Danish con-
ᶠerence held in Copenhagen on April 5-6, 1979. Here
ᴬgain the keynote speaker was a native, Prime Minister

Anker Jorgensen. However, central to the program were Jacques Delors who discussed the notion of worker control espoused by the PS, and Herbert Ehrenberg, German Minister of Labour and Social Affairs.[37] It seems that the pattern was to choose a subject for a particular country's conference which was compatible with the expertise of the national party's leader. Thus, the host party was assured a prominent position. At the same time, notables from other parties provided exposure to varied currents of European socialist thought, and the beginning of an acquaintance with the leaders of the Socialist Group. The conferences received moderate press coverage and were considered a success by their organizers.[38] The Labour Party was the only Confederation member which neither hosted a conference nor sent speakers to the other conferences.

Even Labour, however, attended the April 26, 1979 meeting for socialist candidates in Luxembourg. This event was organized so that the "top of the list" candidates from the Nine, along with Spanish and Portuguese socialist leaders, could meet together. It also provided a forum for the major international leaders to speak. At this session the candidates and the leadership were on their best behavior. One Paris newspaper headlined its coverage with the statement, "The European Socialists are minimizing their differences."[39] Two hundred candidates heard Willy Brandt and Francois Mitterrand affirm socialist unity, and call for further democratization of the Community and reform of the institutions.[40]

Two rallies in France, in Lille in November 1978, and in Paris at the end of May 1979, were also coordinated by the Confederation in cooperation with the Parti Socialiste.[41] The kickoff in Lille had participants from eight of the member countries, as well as Greece, Spain, and Portugal. The conspicuous absentees were the leadership of the British Labour Party, who pleaded the pressure of their parliamentary schedule. Two objectives seem to have motivated the French PS in planning the rally: "to draw attention to the solidarity of Socialist Europe" and to assert the PS's "strength and its dynamism for domestic political consumption."[42] Socialist intellectuals and political notables from several countries, most significantly Willy Brandt, addressed the gathering. The genius behind this event was Jacques Lang of the PS, who was appointed to the Confederation's electoral committee because "the Confederation wanted an attractive, lively campaign."[43]

The Paris rally at the end of the campaign drew the attention of the New York Times. In discussing transnational political compromises of the major groups, Flora Lewis noted:

The Socialists have gone furthest in this effort,

demonstrating cohesion at a huge rally in Paris last weekend despite important differences. They were able to bring together not only the Socialist leaders of all the member states, including Greece, but also of Spain and Portugal.[44]

Perhaps the great coup of this event was the presence of John Prescott of the Labour Party, who even used the occasion to negotiate for some emergency financial support from the Confederation.[45]

Aside from these major events, the Confederation staff had hoped to organize arrangements for the trading of speakers and other types of informal cooperation. Providing transnational speakers was hampered by one simple snag: language. Willy Brandt was a great asset because he is fluent in Danish, French, and Italian, but he is an exception.[46] Apparently, arrangements for speakers also bogged down for technical reasons: the parties, unused to this type of campaign, did not plan sufficiently in advance. The result was that the trading of speakers was based on personal contact rather than central planning.[47]

Several threads run through evaluations of the various campaign efforts of the Confederation. By this point in the study they are familiar. The Confederation was successful either when the constituent parties had given prior agreement to a plan, for example the use of the transnational emblem, or when its work did not require the national elites to become involved, as in the mailing of literature. The conferences took place and were well received in most countries. However, in the United Kingdom, where Labour would allow no such European program, the Confederation had no power to organize independently. National party autonomy clearly overruled transnational planning.

One might also note that the undertakings of the Confederation were modest in scale. The parties had made key decisions which placed primary emphasis on the national level. Pivotal among them was allowing each national party to wage a campaign based on its own manifesto. Thus, while there were some outward signs of transnational socialist unity, each member of the Confederation was free to decide just how much unity would help or hamper its efforts. One might question whether significant integration can occur in this type of situation where national independence carries with it no transnational political penalties.

THE NATIONAL CAMPAIGNS

It was the nature of the first European election campaign that it was primarily conducted on the national level. Despite efforts at coordination on the part of

the transnational party group infrastructures, nine separate campaigns organized around nine separate sets of
national issues were the actuality of spring 1979.
Therefore, in order to ultimately assess the effectiveness of the direct elections to the European Parliament
in generating integrative "spillovers" it is necessary
to analyze the national campaigns of the three parties
under study.

The three campaigns which will be discussed below
differ greatly for a variety of reasons, for example,
national political situations, availability of adequate
funding, and elite attitudes toward the direct elections. Because of the complex interplay of these and
other variables, each campaign took on a distinct character. Our purpose here is to first discuss each of the
three campaigns as the unique event it was, and then to
compare the three according to several specific criteria: elite behavior, possible reasons for motivation or
lack thereof, voter response, and transnational aspects.
This method of analysis should allow for an evaluation
of the neo-functionalist paradigm's explanatory value.

The SPD Campaign: Stereotypical Thoroughness

The German Social Democratic Party conducted a
well-prepared, well-organized, well-financed, pro-
Europe campaign for the European Parliament. The SPD
and the CDU (Christian Democratic Party) are both pro-
Europe parties, so the West German voters were not making a choice about the Community, but about subtle differences in proposed ways to build Europe. The results
of the campaign gave the SPD almost forty-three percent
of the popular vote, just about their average in national elections in the 1970s, but party staff were con-
vinced that low turnout - sixty percent of the eligible - hurt the SPD because voting was lightest in their
traditional strongholds.[48] Discussion of their campaign
will cover educational programs, funding, the campaigning per se, selection of candidates, role of party
leaders, and transnational efforts. An attempt will be
made to interpret their low turnout in light of their
apparently strenuous campaigning.

Funding explains much about what the SPD was able
to do. West German parties receive government funds for
campaigning, and for the European contest the SPD received sixty million Deutschmarks, even without which
they would have been able to draw on a substantial
treasury. The West German parties met together and set
mutually agreed upon spending ceilings because of escalating campaign costs in recent years.[49] Ceiling or
not, the Social Democratic Party was able to support an
elaborate program of publications, media advertising,
and campaign travel. This, of course, gave them a de-

cided advantage over the bankrupt British Labour Party, but not over the German CDU - and that is the only advantage which would have mattered. The SPD was well organized to handle a European campaign long before it became relevant. They have had, for some time, a coordinator for European affairs who works with the Bundestagfraktion and the delegation to the European Parliament, as well as participating in the work of the Socialist Group and Confederation. Helga Köhnen, the coordinator during the campaign, is the expert responsible for the content of most of the major policy and educational documents used, and was available throughout the campaign to assist local party organizations in need of factual knowledge about the Community and Parliament.[50] None of the other parties in the Socialist Group had such a long term permanent staff person to act as a resource at the time of the elections.

Because those charged with carrying out the local campaigns, and the candidates themselves in many instances, had no previous firsthand experience in dealing with Europe, the party took upon itself the task of educating them. This was done through publications and a series of seminars. Argumente für Europa was the key briefing book.[51] Thematic chapters are arranged in question and answer format which allows a prospective speaker to quickly prepare responses which are both factually correct and in keeping with the SPD's nationally articulated positions. Another pamphlet, Dokumente zur Europapolitik, contains the texts of five major SPD policy statements on the Community, enabling candidates to assimilate positions articulated by the party conferences during the five years previous to the election.[52] The third major background document was the election manifesto, Soziale Demokratie für Europa, which was discussed extensively in Chapter Three.[53]

Another resource employed in campaign preparations was the SPD's think-tank, the Friedrich Erburt Foundation.[54] The staff of the foundation conducted a series of seminars concerning European integration for local SPD activists.[55] These seminars, coupled with the publications mentioned above, assured the party of at least a basic knowledge of campaign issues on the part of those who were responsible for managing local efforts.

The list system called for by the Federal Republic's choice of proportional representation for this election allowed the Parteivorstand to set some clear priorities about who would represent the SPD in the directly elected Parliament. A special congress in December 1978 voted out the list, and it was no surprise that the party president, Willy Brandt, was unanimously elected to the first position.[56] Brandt's willingness to stand carried with it one stipulation which affected designation to "safe" places on the list: he demanded that twenty percent of the safe positions be assigned to

women or he would refuse to run.[57] A further decision
concerned the problem of the double mandate. Realizing
the burden of serving in two active parliamentary bodies, yet understanding the need for some continuity of
experience in the European Parliament, the German SPD
opted to allow twenty percent of their candidates a
double mandate. This solution freed several major figures of the appointed Parliament to return, among them
Ludwig Fellermaier who had chaired the Socialist Group
and Erwin Lange who became chair of the new Budget Committee.[58] Important trade union leaders, local party
activists, and party staff filled out the remainder of
the eighty-one positions.

Willy Brandt's role in the campaign was highly significant. At the time of his election to head the list
he pledged that he would "place himself at the entire
disposal of the Party for the European election campaign."[59] The record of his activities demonstrates
that he made good on his pledge, and that he took the
principal role in active campaigning for his party. In
certain instances, television spots and campaign leaflets for example, he and Helmut Schmidt always appeared
together.[60] However, Schmidt was the chancellor and
Brandt was the candidate, and Schmidt's public appearances were reserved for a few major rallies.[61] Brandt's
schedule, as deduced from press releases and copies of
his speeches, took him all over the Federal Republic
during a span of several months. In this effort he was
substantially assisted by Heinz-Oskar Vetter, second on
the list and Germany's most influential trade union
leader.[62] Perhaps it should be repeated here that
Brandt also participated in the French, Italian, and
Danish campaigns. The impact of his role on the overall
campaign is difficult to judge, but it does seem fair to
conclude that he was the most important social democratic figure in both the West German and transnational campaigns.

The SPD campaign had one key goal: to get out the
vote. Party staff judged, quite correctly as it turned
out, that the SPD's natural electorate would not be interested in Europe. Two persons involved in the effort
had slightly different perceptions about lack of interest among the rank and file SPD members. One believes
that working people see Europe as "the affair of the
well-educated," a concern of "the bourgeoisie who always
travel." The other felt that the problem was translating complex issues, particularly those relating to reforms which the SPD advocated, into a language which
average voters could understand.[63]

The problem of getting out the vote was addressed
through a massive publicity campaign which focused, in
contrast to materials prepared for party activists, on
a few basic themes.[64] Perhaps the most emotionally
powerful is a large poster of Brandt and Schmidt with

the heading "We want Europe as a power for peace." The
rest of the text outlines the major initiatives for
peace taken by the SPD under Brandt and Schmidt. Three
other themes dominate the campaign literature: Europe
for the workers, enhancing women's rights through
Europe, and the challenge of building a socialist Eu-
rope.65

Most of the SPD leaflets contained clip-out coupons
with which readers could order a variety of campaign
paraphernalia. It is worth noting that everything offered carried the election symbol of the Confederation.
These same coupons could be used to request copies of
the various in-depth campaign publications. Buttons,
bumper stickers, and books were all available free of
charge.66

Political campaigns often generate at least one
"personality" issue which either overshadows the substantive problems at hand or indirectly calls attention
to them. In this West German contest the issue was the
candidacy of Otto von Habsburg who was third on the
Christian Social Union (CSU, the Bavarian ally of the
CDU) list. In fact, the British and American press
largely ignored the West German campaign, but Dr. Habsburg's candidacy received coverage in the New York Times
and the Financial Times.67 It also gave Brandt and the
SPD a handy target for their attack on the conservative
nature of the opposition. Franz-Josef Strauss, CSU
leader, is by no means mild in his advocacy of rightest
positions, but Habsburg, among other positions, called
for "the European nations to accept that a strong man
should be allowed to take over the government for up to
nine months (suspending all laws) during emergencies,
such as nuclear blackmail."68 The SPD attacked Habsburg
and the party which nominated him in a fifty-five page
publication, one of only four in a series called Europa-
Informationen.69 Much of the text consists of reprints
of Habsburg statements on such matters as white supremacy in South Africa and his views on Adolf Hitler. Because of Habsburg's place on the list his election was
virtually assured, but his presence as a CDU-CSU candidate gave the SPD a clear issue with which to distinguish themselves from their rivals.

The major German parties ran advertisements in
principal German newspapers as an additional means of
gaining support.70 However, my records indicate that
the SPD was the only party to print an ad whose text was
in French. The one page display in Der Spiegel several
days before the election contained a cartoon depicting
children at play. The caption read "Ils font partie de
l'Europe" ("They belong to Europe"). The text quoted
Jean Jacques Sempé, once again in French: "The idea of
Europe gives me hope."71 This gesture in itself proves
little empirically about the SPD's pro-integration sincerity, but it adds to other evidence which demonstrates

that the SPD is committed to the idea of European unity.
The SPD won thirty-five of the eighty-one West German seats in the new Parliament, a ratio which roughly
compares to its strength in the Bundestag at the time,
where they governed in a coalition with the Free Democratic Party (FDP). As mentioned previously, voter
turnout was lowest in SPD strongholds. Although exact
documentation is not available, it would seem that the
SPD made further inroads into the middle class in this
election. Otherwise, they would not have fared as well.
If this was the case, there are three possible causes.
The first, and weakest, is a ripple effect from the much
publicized Habsburg candidacy in Bavaria. The second,
and, I think, principal factor in shoring up the SPD was
the personal charisma of Brandt. Electing a former
chancellor who has immense personal popularity to the
European Parliament, and sending a strong SPD delegation
with him, was one way of insuring continued West German
leadership in the Parliament. A third possible, the
pro-integration stance of the SPD, cannot be weighed too
heavily because the CDU also has an unblemished record
regarding the building of Europe. Whatever the case,
the SPD was somewhat disappointed, but by no means dev-
astated at the polls.[72]
    In summarizing the Social Democratic Party's cam-
paign in the Federal Republic, one quality of that campaign stands out very clearly: it was taken very seriously by the party's leadership. The reasons behind
that fact have pivotal implications for the conclusions
to be eventually drawn in this study. The SPD can point
to its 1925 Heidelberg Program which called for a politically united Europe, but the 1925 party, and in fact
the overall situation in Germany sixty years ago, were
radically different from contemporary realities. The
answer has to lie in the Federal Republic, in West
German perceptions of where the best future lies, and in
the post-Godesberg SPD - or it might lie in a neo-functionalist analysis. The question properly phrased is
whether factors particular to post World War II Germany
are responsible for the SPD's commitment to Europe, or
whether once the SPD became involved in Europe they were
unwittingly swept along by a central dynamic, that is,
spillover.
    Several different perceptions about why the West
Germans take the Community seriously and tend to support
integration are held by Socialist Group members. The
first to be discussed here may be a valid reason, or it
may be a British excuse for Labour's less than positive
record. This argument is based on Germany's political
history in the past century, and postulates that their
institutions have changed so violently several times,
and the Federal Republic is such a young entity, that it
is easier for the Germans than for the British to surrender sovereignty and adjust to new institutions.[73]

The second argument to be advanced is based on a supposed fear held by the West Germans that they have a pathological national character which they must constantly strive to overcome. Stated more concretely, this position articulates a German fear that the country could revert to totalitarianism once again in an unstable political or economic climate. The Community, according to this view, has greatly aided the German "economic miracle" and economic prosperity has strengthened belief in democracy. It would therefore follow that principal West German political leaders, constantly fearful of the "beast" within them and their followers, will work conscientiously to further the aims of the Community.[74]

A third line of reasoning is much less dramatic, but it is espoused by a major figure in German Europolitics. It is simply that the SPD, finding itself a participant in the Community, feels that it ought to play as important a role as possible.[75] Furthermore, given the strength of the SPD within the Federal Republic and its strength relative to the other members of the Socialist Confederation, a leadership role within the Socialist Group and a consequent opportunity to promote the SPD's brand of socialism within the Parliament are within the party's grasp if its efforts are serious.

There is a fourth explanation, this one often offered by European socialists who are both to the left of the German party and hesitant about or opposed to the Community. It is a simple and lucid argument: the SPD, having moved to the right since 1959, is fairly comfortable with the capitalistic thrust of the present Community, and therefore quite willing to operate with good faith within its institutions.[76]

It is an interesting point that the first two of these arguments, which are sweeping in their historical and sociological scope, discuss the German parties across the board, while the last two, which are more narrow and pragmatic, relate specifically to the SPD. It may be that there are kernels of truth in the first analysis, that in fact there is not as much national pride associated with the Bundestag as with Westminster or the National Assembly, and that the Germans have a degree of cautious concern about their democracy. However, Professor Wilhelm Hennis of the University of Freiburg maintains that the real miracle of the Federal Republic is a political one, and that pride in West Germany's recovery of democracy is quite substantial.[77]

The question of the SPD's pro-integration position seems to be best answered by drawing on parts of several of these explanations. First, it is possible that West German tenacity about participation in the Community, the Parliament, and the direct elections is based, not on a fear of losing democracy, but on an eagerness to

128

make it work well. The SPD leadership, in particular,
suffered bitterly under National Socialism, and it is
probable that their enthusiastic participation in German
and European politics is an outgrowth of their historical experience, and not a pathological one. It can also
be argued that it is politically sound for the SPD to
work to strengthen its influence in the Parliament. The
party wants to extend the powers of the Parliament and
they want to increase the influence of pragmatic social
democracy within a bourgeois system which they accept.
Anyone can argue normatively with them, but it was politically intelligent for the SPD, seeing an important
role for itself in the directly elected European Parliament, and viewing the Community as a viable arena for
furthering certain social and economic goals, to fight
persuasively and effectively in the first European campaign. This, they did.

The Parti Socialiste: Presidential Preliminaries

The French Socialist Party's attitude toward the
direct elections to the European Parliament was well articulated by M. Edgar Pisani, MEP, during a 1978 interview in Strasbourg. "The direct election is not in itself a great event," he maintained, "but for the PS it
is a good opportunity to run without the PCF."[78] In
France, more so than in any other major Community state,
the proportional election to the European Parliament assumed its greatest significance as an opportunity for
the principal parties to test the nationwide political
waters almost two years before the 1981 presidential
election.[79] A second characteristic of the French campaign which gives it a unique flair is the ideological
debate which raged among the four major parties and
within the government and the opposition.[80] Jockeying
into position for the two-round presidential election
and debating the fundamentals of Community membership
were important considerations for the PS as its leadership prepared for the spring 1979 campaign. These factors which permeated the entire French campaign will be
discussed here as the content which shaped the PS campaign in terms of publicity, elite activity, campaign
events, and transnational cooperation.

It was presumed in 1979 that the leaders of
France's four major political groupings, Jacques Chirac
of the Gaullists (RPR), President Giscard d'Estaing of
the Union for French Democracy (UDF), Francois Mitterrand of the PS, and Georges Marchais of the PCF, would
compete in the 1981 presidential election. If past patterns held in this election, during the second round of
voting the parties of the left and of the right would
unite behind the candidate from their "side" who exhib-

ited the most strength in the first round. Therefore, the parties were interested in analyzing two sets of percentages in the European election results: the right-left breakdown defined as RPR-UDF totals contrasted with the combined PS-PCF vote, and the strength of each of the four parties vis-à-vis its "natural" coalition part-ner.[81] In other words, there was a perceived opportuni-ty to measure which side had the strongest position, and which candidates would most likely contest the second round. This situation alone was seen as important e-nough for the three people who wanted to succeed Giscard to head their parties' lists. Giscard's UDF, not to be outdone in the popularity contest, placed the very pop-ular minister Simone Veil at the head of their list.[82]

The presidential opinion poll aspect of the cam-paign, and efforts by Chirac to turn the election into a referendum on the Giscard-Barre government,[83] were com-plicated, if not muddled, by substantive debate between the left and right parties concerning the Community it-self. The two parties of the extremes, Chirac's Gaul-lists and Marchais' PCF, campaigned on strong national-istic and anti-Community platforms, albeit for different reasons, but nevertheless creating a situation noted by John Palmer of the Guardian: "There are times when it is difficult to tell Mr. Chirac and the Communist leader, Mr. Georges Marchais, apart in their European policy statements."[84] Meanwhile, the UDF and the Socialist Party presented moderately pro-integration positions to the voters.[85] The campaigning which resulted from this line-up caused Palmer to comment that "The gladiatorial contest is bloodier within the Majority and Opposition than between them."[86]

The campaign which took place against this backdrop was relatively short, formally beginning on May 26 and concluding with the June 10 vote. Eleven lists of eighty-one candidates each competed, although the four major parties were clearly dominant.[87] Public funding was available to all parties, but was under the French system which requires a deposit of one hundred thousand francs at the time a party registers its list, and then provides three hundred thousand francs to any party which captures at least five percent of the total vote.[88] This financing method practically insured that such small groups as the ecologists and Eurodroite could not mount effective campaigns.

Neither French election laws nor the regulations of the Parti Socialiste precluded a double mandate, which fact allowed prominent members of the party to compete. Mitterrand, as was mentioned, led the Socialist Party's list, but was by no means the only notable guaranteed a seat in Strasbourg. Among the top twenty-five names were Pierre Mauroy, then mayor of Lille, Edith Cresson, Jacques Moreau, Jacques Delors, and Edgar Pisani - all prominent leaders of the party, several with strong

130

reputations throughout the Confederation of Socialist
Parties.[89] It is interesting to note one similarity
with the SPD list: five of the twenty-five presumably
"safe" positions, or twenty percent of the guaranteed
seats, were held by women. The PS women had also fought
for thirty percent of the total eighty-one positions,
and the party, with a strong position favoring women's
rights, had complied.[90]
    One further point about the French election law
should be noted as this galaxy of PS notables are cited
as candidates for the European Parliament. Winners in
the election were allowed to step down and let the next
person on the list occupy their seat. Mitterrand did so
on June 20, ostensibly to protest an unfavorable ruling
on a contested seat.[91] It seems that the nature of the
French political situation in 1979 almost required party
leaders to head their lists and take the role of chief
campaigner. Otherwise, the election as a presidential
popularity contest would have lost much of its validity.
    Active participation by Mitterrand was also re-
quired because of the role Giscard designed for himself
in the campaign. With Mme. Veil, probably his most popular minister, heading the UDF list, he could afford to
project the image of national leader above the fray in a
campaign which he contended had no domestic consequences
for France.[92] Meanwhile, with the UDF ahead in the pre-
election polling and anxious for a large turnout, Giscard inaugurated a "neutral" publicity campaign on government owned television and other media.[93] This media
blitz, which Mitterrand characterized as "massive, ex-
cessive, official propaganda," was attacked by Gaullists
and communists as well, but to no avail.[94]
    Mitterrand's position in the campaign was thus a
difficult one, because it was against Giscard that he
had to appear strong. The problem was heightened by the
fact that the parties headed by both men were waging the
campaign on very similar issues. True, the Socialist
Party was arguing for the advent of a "Europe of the
Workers" while the Giscardiens found little fault with
the present structure and policies, but on such fundamental issues as granting sovereignty to the European
Parliament, something neither party wanted to do at the
time, they found themselves in agreement.[95]
    The actual campaigning of the PS was activist, pos-
itive about the future of the Community, and transnational in both tone and substance. The kickoff rally in
Lille in November 1978, which was mentioned in discussing the Confederation's campaign efforts, was a proto-
type of the events which followed it. International socialist leaders, theatrical and literary personalities,
and an almost carnival-like atmosphere were used by the
PS to generate positive public reaction to the idea of a
socialist future for Europe.[96]
    During spring 1979 Mitterrand and the other top of

the list candidates were traveling extensively in
France and other Community states, yet it should be
noted that every major party in France was conducting an
energetic campaign. On Saturday May 5, for example,
Mitterrand took part in a major rally in Marseilles
which was built around the theme of women's struggle for
equal rights. He used this occasion to announce a major
voter mobilization effort by the PS, in which every local party activist was to receive detailed instructions
from the national leadership for getting out the vote
on June 10.[97] Another important PS rally was organized
in Strasbourg, this one also on a Saturday, May 25. Its
theme was "Europe of the Left." Mitterrand was joined
here, as at other major events, by the best known candidates on the list, as well as by Maurice Faure of the
Left Radicals (MRG) who ran in coalition with the Parti
Socialiste.[98] A third major campaign event was held in
Paris on May 16. This time the occasion was an overview
of five years of Giscardism, but the speeches were primarily concerned with strengthening European socialism
through the Community.[99]

The largest and splashiest event in the French
socialist campaign was also the big unity rally of the
Confederation. The event, called "Printemps Socialiste
de l'Europe" and was both a political and cultural occasion. Every major figure in the Confederation was present - in itself a cause for celebration - and their
joint press conference was well covered by the French
media.[100] The central activity was a concert of classi-
cal and political music at the Place du Trocadero, at
which Melina Mercouri(PASOK) presided and Mitterrand and
Willy Brandt addressed the assembly.[101] This finalé to
the campaign not only projected a unified image for the
Socialist Confederation, it also provided Mitterrand
with a certain international stature in full view of the
French electorate.

The leaders of the Parti Socialiste consistently
participated in international forums, and campaigned for
other socialists from the Nine. Edgar Pisani, noting
several months before the campaign began that he had already agreed to speak in Belgium and Italy, and was in-
viting some colleagues to France, provided some interesting reasons for this travel. He maintained that underlying socialist unity was certainly important, but
educating voters about Community-wide problems the Confederation members wanted to address was an equally viable reason. He wanted French voters to understand that
their economic difficulties were not "French problems,"
and therefore required a broader arena than France in
which to work out solutions.[102]

French participation in the Confederation's seminars and the fact that the PS hosted a seminar on Europe
and the new industrial revolution were previously noted.[103] Jacques Delors, who headed the party's interna-

tional economic relations committee, was frequently on
the road as his party's spokesperson.[104] Mitterrand
made one trip abroad which was particularly notable.
When the British Labour Party finally decided at the
Paris rally in May that they wanted Confederation assistance in conducting a final rally in Leeds, Mitterrand
agreed to join Mr. Callaghan as one of the principal
speakers.[105] To address British voters on the solidarity of European socialism after witnessing Labour's behavior throughout the campaign simply has to be assessed
as a generous gesture of that solidarity!
    The French press played a lively and important role
in the campaign. No doubt because of pre-presidential
politics and the often caustic debate among France's
major political figures, there was no dearth of campaign
coverage by the leading dailies in France. While this
observation is not based on a quantitative comparative
study, it seems that the French press covered the campaign in much greater detail than their British and even
West German counterparts. Along with detailed reports
on campaign activity and commentaries by political scientists, several of the major newspapers ran series of
lengthy interviews with the leaders of all eleven
lists.[106] Particularly during the week preceeding the
voting, such newspapers as Le Monde, Le Figaro, and Le
Soir were carrying page after page of daily coverage.[107]
For any French voter who was a newspaper reader it was
impossible to ignore the first direct elections to the
European Parliament. For those who wished to be well
informed, vast quantities of materials were readily
available.
    One brief observation about a feature which was ab-
sent from the French campaign is necessary for the analysis which is to follow. Whereas the SPD ran an extensive educational program for its candidates and local
activists, there appeared to be no such effort on the
part of the PS in the midst of an otherwise energetic
and positive campaign. The West German campaign was typ-
ified above as an event which was taken very seriously
by the major parties. Considering the discussion of the
French campaign on the preceeding pages, one cannot conclude that the spring of 1979 was any less serious for
the major French political parties, particularly the PS.
However, it is possible to conclude that the reasons underlying the conscientious campaigning of the SPD and PS
were very dissimilar.
    The Parti Socialiste is opposed to any extension of
the powers of the European Parliament under Europe's
present economic and social structures.[108] They campaigned energetically under the theme "Pour Europe des
Travailleurs," yet should have known that the European
Parliament, without a majority on the left working together and without legislative powers, is unable to create a Europe of the workers. The extent of their ef-

forts in this campaign cannot be explained in terms of their hopes for the Parliament. The lack of educational programs, which would probably go unnoticed except for the German SPD, is another thread reaching toward the same conclusion. The campaign and victory in this election were certainly important for the French Socialist Party, but it can be asserted that winning was much more important to the PS than what they would do in the European Parliament after the victory. That is not to say that Mitterrand and his party were not at all concerned about the Parliament, but that effective parliamentary activity in Europe was not their primary goal.[109] Certainly, they made great efforts to be "good Europeans" both in their national campaign and in Confederation activities. However, it seems that their primary purpose was to test their electoral strength in France.

As was noted at the outset of this chapter, the Gaullists and PCF did not fare as well as they had hoped to in the European election. Their extreme nationalism and intransigence about the Community were cited as plausible explanations for their poor showing. Pro-Europe parties ran best in countries where other parties took a negative approach toward the Community. In France there are two major pro-Europe parties with many similar positions on the future of the Community. In 1979 one was led by the president of France and one was led by the man thought most likely to defeat him in 1981 if the presidency changed hands. This single factor is the key to understanding the French campaign.

Giscard d'Estaing did his best to place himself above the European campaign, while doing all in his power to insure that his party would do well in an election he refused to acknowledge as a plebescite on the leadership of France.[110] Francois Mitterrand did not have the Élysées Palace from which to operate, and he was therefore faced with running for the Parliament and evoking as well as possible the historical and contemporary support the Socialist Party has demonstrated toward the Community. This support has been substantial since the Community's inception, and Mitterrand's party had a solid base from which to draw in their European campaign. The pertinent fact is that this history allowed them to mount an effective effort against Giscard and the UDF.

To conclude this treatment of the campaign of the Parti Socialiste: it was ambitious, well-orchestrated, and pro-integration. It was also well received by the French electorate, and in French politics that meant two things: Mitterrand emerged as the stronger left presidential candidate, and the majority of French voters of the left were not opposed to French membership in the Community. The French PS did not, according to all available data, participate enthusiastically in this campaign as an automatic response to a spillover dynamic.

They did so because it was politically wise for them, and their success in the first European elections mattered more to them because of what it signified for 1981, not what occurred in June 1979.

The Labour Campaign: Purposeful Neglect?

The British Labour Party lost a general election to Margaret Thatcher and the Tories only five weeks before the European contest. With drained resources and injured morale they had to face another election - this time to a parliament they will not call a parliament, representing citizens of an organization to which many of them would prefer not to belong. Their European campaign was a disaster both nationally and transnationally. Sarcastic abuse can be heaped upon them only too easily. Rather than taking that route, the following pages will deal with two questions: how did Labour conduct its first European campaign, and why was its performance so dismal and intransigent?

As was discussed extensively in Chapter Two, the Labour Party was not controlled by pro-Marketeers at the time of the direct election. The NEC had opposed entrance into the Community and they campaigned vigorously against the 1975 referendum on renegotiated terms of British membership. The party was also on record as opposed to direct elections to the Parliament. They can be faulted with creating one of the major delays in the election process by insisting on direct representation in single member districts, and consequently having to draw up eighty-one Euro-constituencies.[111] Furthermore, the anti-Marketeers were riding high in spring 1979 after James Callaghan lost the prime ministry and Tony Benn solidified his power on the NEC and the NEC's power over the parliamentary party.[112] This history of relationship with the Community colored the Labour campaign just as surely as differing histories affected the French and German pre-election activities. Questions of how the Labour Party campaigned must be answered by examining their behavior in the spring of 1979, but the answers should be viewed as recent pages in a long history of antagonism toward European integration on the part of certain elements within Labour, elements almost sure to be stronger in the 1984 European election.

Financing became a major problem in the Labour campaign for one simple reason: they had no money.[113] British campaigns are not publicly funded, and in the year before the European election Labour was required to spend on the devolution referendum and the general election, and they had not anticipated the latter would take place as early as spring 1979.[114] However, it can be argued that Transport House neither made efforts to amass a European election fund nor made full use of re-

sources from the Socialist Group, so the poverty defense
put forth by the NEC to explain its paltry efforts on
behalf of the Euro-candidates rings somewhat hollow. At
any rate, very little was spent by the national party
either to encourage a high Labour turnout or to educate
the rank and file about the Community.
  Two incidents reveal the extent to which the Labour
Party leadership failed to maximize available resources.
The first is a small scandal which evolved around the
printing of brochures for each candidate. The brochures, with three pages of text about the party's European election manifesto and one page on the individual
candidate, were paid for with funds from the Confederation. Not only was the text strongly anti-Community,
but because of one mildly pro-Community phrase millions
of these leaflets were scrapped and a whole new batch
printed. It seems the first printing bore the title
"Labour for Europe." That was too much for the NEC and
they ordered the wording changed to "Labour and Europe."[115]
  The second incident occurred when the NEC did send
its "top of the list" people to the Confederation's
conference for candidates in Luxembourg. Many Labour
candidates had been spending their own money on campaign
materials,[116] and they were furious when they discovered that Labour had not used all the funds made available by the Confederation for printing or for an informational seminar. They wrote to Ron Hayward, the General Secretary, and consequently received some funds
for posters. A second result was that John Prescott was
dispatched to the Paris rally where he negotiated for
funds for the rally in Leeds at which Francois Mitterrand spoke.[117]
  Campaign materials produced by Labour were neglig-
ible. The leaflet already discussed, a small flyer
which proclaimed "Labour stands up for Britian," and
copies of the Appeal to the Electorate with a foreward
stating that it was "not a statement of party policy"
were the only materials for general distribution. The
Labour manifesto and a campaign handbook, The EEC, which
was prepared for the general election, were available
for purchase from Transport House.[118] Anything further
used by individual candidates was prepared and financed
by them.
  The role of elites in Labour's campaign was affected from the outset by two factors: the single member
district electoral system and the NEC decision to pro-
hibit a double mandate. Thus, there was no top of the
list candidate to take the national leadership in campaigning, as Mitterrand and Brandt did for their parties. The closest Labour came to a person able to assume such a role was Barbara Castle, one leading MP who
was willing to give up her seat in Commons in order to
run for Europe. However, even though Mrs. Castle was

considered the front-runner in the Greater Manchester
North Euro-district, there is no such thing as a sure
seat under district representation, and she had to campaign effectively among her own constituents.[119] Therefore, she was not free to travel extensively in support
of other Labour candidates, and because a vote for another candidate did not help to send Barbara Castle to
Europe, her personal popularity did little to aid Labour
outside of Manchester. Battles between Tony Benn and
James Callaghan about whether Labour should have contested the election and on the content of the European
manifesto, which raged for over a year before the election, and the power plays that placed Benn and his allies in charge of the campaign, were all rather effective in preventing Callaghan from taking an active public role in the campaign.[120] Of course, the loss of the
general election further diminished Callaghan's effectiveness.

The situation for the Tories was different for several reasons. They permitted the double mandate and
therefore had more candidates with whom the voters were
familiar. They also had the services of a popular elder
statesman, Edward Heath, who campaigned in forty-one
constituencies, delivered thirty-five major speeches,
and made scores of informal appearances.[121] Lastly,
they were able to present themselves as the constructive, pro-Europe party in contrast to the squabbling
leadership of Labour.

The British press, although its coverage did not
equal the breadth of French reporting, was attentive to
the campaign and generally supportive of the direct e-
lections. This attitude and the tongue-in-cheek style
of many British journalists did little to improve Labour's credibility. Headlines such as "Mr. Benn aims
Labour at the EEC,"[122] and "Roll up that map of Europe,"[123] were typical of articles reporting on the Labour campaign. Editorials in the days immediately preceeding June 7 encouraged the public to vote, and tried
to emphasize the importance of the Parliament.[124] It
may be argued that the positive attitude of the press
was of more help to the Conservatives than to Labour
because it highlighted the poor attempt made by Labour
in its campaigning.

Opinion polling is a major occupation in Great
Britain at election time, and the pollsters were busy in
spring 1979. Their tabulations in the weeks before the
election did not bode well for Labour, and in fact
caused an upswing in the party's electoral efforts as
the campaign closed. David Butler and David Marquand
had been working with the Labour Party and had produced
a list of thirty-five to forty winable seats based on
patterns in the 1974 general election.[125] If 1979 general election results had been replicated, Labour's
candidates would have won twenty-nine seats on June

7.126 However, as the campaign wound toward its conclusion the Labour Party was panicked by a second set of
polls, these predicting very low voter turnout. In late
May only twenty-eight percent of the British questioned
said they definitely intended to vote, and it was the
prevailing political wisdom that a low turnout would
heighten the Tory advantage.[127]
In the final weeks before the election both Ron
Hayward and James Callaghan wrote letters to the Labour
candidates encouraging them to do their best to get out
the vote in their districts. The NEC even sent prepared
press releases to the candidates for distribution to
local newspapers.[128] The releases covered two themes:
Britain's raw deal from the Community, and the dangers
of "Thatcherism" spreading to the Community. These
press releases were part of an effort to clear up voter
confusion resulting from Labour's anti-Community campaign. It was feared that this negative approach would
discourage unsophisticated voters from going to the
polls. These last efforts gave Tony Benn and Michael
Foot sufficient assurance to predict at Labour's June 6
news conference that the Labour vote could be much larger than anticipated by the press, and that since the
campaign had taken off "Voters understood the party's
European policy in which all countries would co-operate
on the basis of national self-government."[129]
Last minute predictions put the expected turnout at
forty percent, and they were overly optimistic.[130] Only
thirty-one percent of the United Kingdom's electorate
participated, and over half of them voted Conservative.
Labour's forty-four percent of the vote gave the party
only seventeen seats in the directly elected Parliament.
It was commented in the British press that the sixty
elected Tories were going to Europe with the support of
a mere sixteen percent of the eligible voters.[131] Public response was much more apathetic than anticipated,
and this apathy was most damaging to Labour.
The transnational aspects of the British campaign
have already been alluded to several times, and need
only brief mention here. The Labour Party was a major
obstacle to Confederation plans to organize the European
campaign around a common platform, and continued its
pattern of recalcitrance throughout the campaign. Labour used Confederation funds to print strongly worded
anti-integration campaign materials. The NEC refused to
have a candidates' seminar in the UK or to send British
speakers to seminars on the continent. Until the candidates attacked Ron Hayward for his failure to obtain
available assistance from the Socialist Confederation,
the party - while pleading destitution - had not even
taken full advantage of Confederation plans for aiding
national parties. The Leeds rally which the Confederation financed was brought about more because of pressure
from candidates than because of NEC plans to wage an ef-

fective campaign.

Fairness to the Labour Party requires one to consider that they had to conduct the most important weeks of their European campaign at a time when they were trying to recover from their defeat at the hands of Margaret Thatcher. The difficulty of fighting a general election campaign and the European campaign at the same time cannot be written off. However, it is evident from the record that the NEC had balked on planning and executing a serious Euro-campaign long before it was known that there would be a parliamentary election in April 1979, and certainly far in advance of knowledge of their defeat in that election. The situation they found themselves in during May was certainly not favorable to a strong Labour showing on June 7, but it is simplistic and short-sighted to blame low morale alone for Labour's debacle.

The National Executive Committee of the Labour Party can be quite justifiably held responsible for a series of actions which contributed to Labour's resounding defeat in the European election. Until April of 1978 they were resolute in their statements that Labour would not even contest the election. Thus, while some of their European colleagues were already planning, Labour was standing still. Their decision regarding the double mandate also seems to have been an error of political judgment because the Tories and the leading continental parties all permitted at least some of their experienced European parliamentarians to run for the directly elected Parliament. True, the double mandate places burdens on those who hold it, but the decision to forbid it probably hurt the Labour Party politically. Unwillingness to fully take advantage of assistance offered by the Confederation seems to have been plain foolishness if lack of adequate funds was really the NEC's reason for not going all out in the campaign.

In discussing the relatively successful campaigns of the PS and SPD, it was not difficult to analyze the reasons behind their efforts. An attempt to discover why Labour took the route it did in the European campaign is more complex because some of the Labour Party's decisions do not seem to reflect good sense on one important level: it is the business of political parties to win elections. This is not to say that Labour should have adopted a pro-integration strategy, but rather that it is puzzling that experienced politicians were so blatantly ineffectual in managing a campaign, and almost purposely so.

The leaders of the Confederation of Socialist Parties were well aware that voter turnout would be pivotal to their overall success.[132] Most Confederation activities during the campaign were planned as a means of interesting the socialist voters in the direct elections. Yet, the Labour Party, which argues that Community membership has adverse effects on British workers, did very little to convince these workers to vote Labour and demonstrate their support of this position on June 7. Party leadership argued that they had insufficient funds, yet full use was not made of resources which were available, and in fact large sums were wasted on reprinting the basic campaign brochure.

The NEC's grudging indecision about contesting the election is also curious. True, Labour was on record as opposed to the direct election of the European Parliament. However, most European political observers had concluded that the European results would have implications within each state. Therefore, even if the Labour Party did not want to campaign for Europe, some thought should have been given to the possible national political consequences of a disaster at the polls. And even when the decision to participate was made, it seems that Ron Hayward and Tony Benn, in particular, did all in their power to wreck Labour's chances. In fact, it is strongly rumored that the NEC worked to block the candidacy of several pro-Europe Labourites who had national followings.[133] The anit-Marketeers did not want to run, but they were not about to let the pro-Marketeers go to Strasbourg.

One speculation about Labour's conduct vis-à-vis Europe in 1979 is based on the brief time span the British party had spent in the Confederation and the Parliament. Labour took no part in either organization until after the British referendum on Community membership in 1975. Therefore, one could postulate that the British - over twenty years behind their continental colleagues - had been insufficiently socialized at the European level when the direct elections became an issue. History, however, dampens the argument. The SPD opposed the ECSC, but its members took their place in the Common Assembly and worked constructively from the start. The Labour Party, on the other hand, purposely absented itself from Brussels and Strasbourg during Britain's early years of membership. The anti-Europe attitude of the NEC cannot be solely attributed to a lack of socialization.

Only one possible conclusion about the Labour Party's role in the direct elections has sufficient evidence to support it: Labour is so firmly opposed to any acquisition of sovereignty on the part of the European Parliament that its leadership purposely and knowingly ran its campaign in such a manner as to undercut any growth in stature for the Parliament or its elected members. The decision not to allow MPs to run for Europe, attempts to block pro-integration candidates, the failure to raise campaign funds, and the neglect of available Confederation resources all point to the validity of such a conclusion. One can assume that the leadership of the Labour Party is in outright opposition to

the European idea, and that no amount of interaction at
the European level is about to trick them into trans-
nationalism. It is difficult to establish any defensi-
ble reason for their poor conduct of the campaign, except that they found it very important to make the European elections very unimportant.

CONCLUSION

The first European elections took place on June 7
and 10, 1979, as scheduled, and their results sent 410
directly elected Members of the European Parliament to
Strasbourg. The event in itself is historic. Whether
the interest generated by the campaigns, or the voter
turnout, or even the political clout of the new Parliament measure up to the hopes of the pro-Europeans, the
fact remains that the Community was able to push formal
integration one major step forward.

Neo-functionalism, however, rests its analysis on
the informal aspects of the integration process. The
question a neo-functionalist must ask is not whether the
obligations of each state to conduct the elections were
met, but whether the process of the elections had any
impact on elite commitment to the Community. Was the
direct election campaign a learning process with positive outcomes in terms of integrative attitudes among
political party leadership?

In answering that question, one must first acknowledge that there were two levels in this campaign and
that it was not infrequent for them to totally miss each
other. The Commission's information campaign and the
coordination efforts on the part of the transnational
political groups were designed and orchestrated by committed pro-integrationists, most of whom worked directly
for the Community. The Commission's campaign was
pitched at a level far removed from national or transnational political issues. Its purpose was to evoke a
sense of being "European" which would result in high
voter turnout. It was, in this sense, very neo-functionalist. That is, it bypassed national governments
and attempted to appeal to politically active individuals on the basis of commitment to a vague ideal, rather
than on the basis of issues. As previously cited, the
Euro-barometer poll demonstrated a higher level of voter
awareness about the direct election in all nine electorates after the information campaign, so the Commission
considered its efforts successful.[134] It seems reason-
able to conclude that the Commission's information campaign was necessary because voters had to be motivated
toward participation in a new process. However, it is
difficult to assess the impact of the publicity campaign
because it took place simultaneously with national pre-
electoral activities, and because there was such a wide

disparity among the nine polities in actual voting. While the Commission was motivated by a desire to involve citizens in the integration project, thus strengthening its base, the Socialist Group was motivated by a desire to maximize its representation in the directly elected Parliament. The key to its success was also high voter turnout because this, as known from past trends, meant a larger proportion of working class votes.[135] The Socialist Group had both advantages and disadvantages the Commission did not possess. Their advantage was that they were able to take partisan positions and thus ask voters for something. They were able to "appeal to the electorate." However, the disadvantages faced by the Socialist Group's European core were substantial. They were not able to bypass the national parties, but had to work through their bureaucracies and with their candidates. Hence, through the Confederation they were able to assist those member parties who approached the campaign with good will and enthusiasm, but their hands were tied in Great Britain where the party officials clearly did not want their help or advice. They were not an independent force in the campaign, but one which was clearly dependent upon each Confederation member. As such, the extent of their success varied tremendously among constituent parties, although the responsibility for this unevenness is not theirs.

The three major national-level socialist campaigns were distinctly different in character, in motivation, and in results at the polls. The French and West German parties literally threw themselves into their campaigns, and while neither produced an overwhelming victory they were both able to send respectably-sized delegations to the new European Parliament. Both of these national contingents had among their members some experienced and committed European Parliamentarians. The Labour Party, in stark contrast, ran a poor campaign with embarrassing results. Most of its newly elected delegation were not only inexperienced at the European level, but had never served in any parliamentary body.[136]

It is not the purpose here to argue with the leadership of the Labour Party, but to demonstrate that national independence was the major factor in this campaign. The structure of the Community, the powers possessed by its Parliament, even the electoral system employed in this first European contest, all contributed to each national party's freedom of action. If, for national reasons, a particular party was not motivated to make a major effort at the European level, there were few transnational rewards to induce it to do so. The SPD apparently takes great pride in its constructive role in the European Parliament, and therefore approached its European campaign with great seriousness of purpose. The French Parti Socialiste, which has a long record of pro-Community positions, was additionally - if

not primarily - motivated by the need to demonstrate
that it was a strong and responsible party within
France. Hence, the PS took maximum advantage of the opportunity provided by the first European elections. The
British Labour Party, or at least those who wield power
within it, disagrees fundamentally with the idea of
European integration, and opposes any activity which can
enhance the credibility of the Community or its Parliament. The lesson of this campaign is that the present
structure of the Community is not compatible with bringing in those national elites who have chosen to oppose
the integration project.

The structure which exists was designed according
to the neo-functionalist model as the best means to
gradually lead elites into a new set of loyalties.[137]
Community participation is thus a school of integration,
and any change in the Community's method of functioning
is evaluated in terms of its effect on elite attitudes.
Therefore, for those who favor the evolution of the Community into a federal Europe, the long term importance
of the first direct election is its role as a device for
building new elite ties with the center. The question
of whether the Community, designed according to the neo-
functionalist method, is capable of creating such links
will be taken up in the next chapter.

NOTES

1. "Nine Nation Parliament must build an image,"
International Herald Tribune, June 12, 1979. It should
be noted that a few seats were contested in several
countries, so reports of exact results occasionally differ according to one's source.
2. "Vote for European Parliament Sets Back Socialists, Shows Nations' Internal Battles," Wall Street
Journal, June 12, 1979.
3. "Conservatives Gain in Europe's Voting," New
York Times, June 12, 1979.
4. Helga Köhnen, interview, Palais de l'Europe,
Strasbourg, France, Oct. 24, 1979.
5. "L'Europe Frileuse," Le Matin (Paris), June 12,
1979. All translations from French and German are by
the author unless otherwise noted.
6. See, for example, New York Times, June 12, 1979,
and J.O. Goldsborough, "410 Elected," Europe (July-Aug.
1979), p. 7.
7. Goldsborough, "410 Elected," p. 7.
8. "Nine Nation Parliament Must Build an Image."
9. The Economist, April 21, 1979, Frankfurter
Allgemeine Zeitung, June 6, 1979, Le Monde, June 6, 1979,
Le Monde Internationale, May 24, 1979, Der Spiegel, May
21, 1979, and Die Zeit, June 8, 1979, provide good ex-

amples of this coverage.

10. <u>Europe</u> Press Release no. 2696, June 11-12, 1979; Socialist Group File, Library, Commission of the European Communities Delegation to the United Nations, New York N.Y.

11. ibid.

12. Paul Zahn, "The Advertising Campaign," <u>Europe</u> (July-Aug. 1979), p. 5.

13. <u>The European Parliament</u>(Luxembourg: General Secretariat of the European Parliament, June 1978). I am on several Community mailing lists. At present I possess 18 copies of this leaflet in 5 languages. Obviously, everyone was using it.

14. These materials may be obtained from European Community information offices, Rue de la Loi, 244, Brussels, and 61 rue des Belles-Feuilles, Paris.

15. Zahn, "Advertising Campaign," p. 5.

16. "Euro-barometer No. 8," European Parliament File, Library, Commission of the European Communities, New York, N.y.

17. <u>European Community News</u>, May 15, 1979.

18. It was expected that voter turnout in the UK and the Netherlands, in particular, would be much higher.

19. Edgar Pisani, interview, Palais de l'Europe, Strasbourg, France, Nov. 15, 1978.

20. Köhnen, Oct. 24, 1979.

21. Examples are the candidacy of Otto von Habsburg in Bavaria, and the European election's perceived impact on the French presidential elections. Both are discussed later in this chapter.

22. Confidential interview, Palais de l'Europe, Strasbourg, Oct. 25, 1979.

23. <u>Europe</u> Press Release no. 2477, June 26-27, 1978. Samples may be obtained from the Confederation of Socialist Parties, 24 Place de la Justice, Brussels.

24. <u>L'Humanité</u> (Paris), June 26, 1978.

25. These are obtainable through the Confederation at the address cited above, at the Community's New York Library, or directly from the national parties.

26. According to Jan Kurleman, interviewed on Nov. 15, 1978 at the Palais de l'Europe, Aicher has been a popular figure within the SPD. Also of interest, Aicher designed all graphics for the 1972 Munich Olympics.

27. Walter Brown, interview, Transport House, London, Nov. 1, 1978.

28. See Zahn, "The Advertising Campaign."

29. These can be obtained on a regular basis by writing to the Socialist Group of the European Parliament, 3, Bd. de l'Empereur, 1000 Brussels.

30. "European Elections: A New Opportunity for Women?" <u>European Socialist</u>, No. 2 (Feb. 1979).

31. "Xth Congress of the Confederation of Socialist Parties of the European Communities," <u>European Socialist</u>

No. 3, (March 1979).
    32. "Specialized Conferences of the Confederation of the Socialist Parties of the European Communities," European Socialist No. 4 (April 1979).
    33. It should be noted that the three issues of European Socialist cited above deal not with the work of the Socialist Group in the Parliament, but with the Confederation's campaign. Community funds are regularly used for political purposes.
    34. Much of my information on these conferences was acquired while interviewing Jan Kurleman, Nov. 15, 1978.
    35. Michael Wood, interview, Palais de l'Europe, Strasbourg, Oct. 24, 1979.
    36. Europe Press Release, no. 2578, Dec. 11-12, 1978.
    37. European Socialist, April 1979, p. 9.
    38. Kurleman was most enthusiastic about their success when I spoke with him in Oct. 1979.
    39. La Croix (Paris), April 28, 1979.
    40. ibid. Also see Euro Report, no. 590, April 28, 1979, Socialist Group file, European Community Library, New York.
    41 Manchester Guardian Weekly, Nov. 19, 1978, Times (London), Nov. 8, 1978, New York Times, June 6, 1979.
    42. Times (London), Nov. 8, 1978.
    43. Kurleman, Nov. 15, 1978.
    44. New York Times, June 6, 1979.
    45. Confidential interview, Palais de l'Europe, Strasbourg, Oct. 25, 1979.
    46. Kurleman, Oct. 24, 1979.
    47. Köhnen, Oct. 24, 1979.
    48. ibid.
    49. ibid.
    50. Ms. Köhnen, Coordinator for European Questions in the SPD Bundestagfraktion, attends all meetings of the European Parliament, the Socialist Group, and the Confederation, and acts as a liason between these organizations and the SPD's national leadership.
    51. SPD, Argumente für Europa (Bonn: Vorstand der SPD, Feb. 1979). This and other SPD election materials may be obtained from the SPD Information Office, Erich Ollenhauerhaus, Bonn-Bad Godesberg.
    52. SPD, Dokumente zur Europapolitik (Bonn: Vorstand der SPD, 1978).
    53. SPD, Soziale Demokratie für Europa (Bonn: Vorstand der SPD, 1979.
    54. The Friedrich-Erburt Foundation, Adenaueralle, Bonn-Bad Godesberg.
    55. Köhnen, Oct. 24, 1979.
    56. Europe Press Release, no. 2578, Dec. 11-12, 1978.
    57. Köhnen, Oct. 24, 1979.
    58. This decision contrasts sharply with Labour Party policy, the result of which was that every member

of the Labour delegation to the directly elected Parliament was inexperienced in Europe, and most had no previous parliamentary experience at all.
59. <u>Europe</u> Press Release, no. 2578, Dec. 11-12, 1978.
60. See for example, SPD, <u>Sagt Ja zu Europa</u> (Bonn: Vorstand der SPD, 1979).
61. Schmidt appeared at two major rallies, in Nuremberg on May 20, 1979, and in Hanover on May 26, 1979. See SPD, <u>Sagt Ja zu Europa</u>.
62. Egon Bahr. ed., SPD Press Service, Ollenhauerstrasse, Bonn.
63. Köhnen and Kurleman, Oct. 24, 1979.
64. The SPD conducted an extensive television campaign which I did not see because I was not in Europe during the months immediately preceeding the election. Printed materials were obtained from the SPD Vorstand, Erich Ollenhauerhaus, Bonn.
65. See SPD, <u>Sagt Ja zu Europa</u>, <u>Frauen für Europa</u>, <u>Arbeitnehmer fordern das Soziale Europa</u> (Bonn: Vorstand der SPD, 1979).
66. For example, the leaflet <u>Soziale Europa</u> contains a coupon with which one could order copies of the SPD's European election manifesto, several informative booklets, and a variety of publicity materials, all in large quantities if desired.
67. <u>New York Times</u>, May 21, 1979, and <u>Financial Times</u> (London), June 7, 1979.
68. <u>Financial Times</u>, June 7, 1979.
69. SPD, <u>Europa-Informationen: Quellen zu Otto von Habsburg</u> (Bonn: Vorstand der SPD, 1979).
70. See, for example, the FDP's advertisement in the <u>Frankfurter Allgemeine Zeitung</u>, June 7, 1979.
71. <u>Der Spiegel</u>, June 4, 1979.
72. Flora Lewis, "Conservatives Gain in Europe's Voting," <u>New York Times</u>, June 12, 1979.
73. Baron Edward Castle, interview, House of Lords, London, Nov.1, 1978
74. Confidential interview, Strasbourg, Nov. 16, 1978.
75. Köhnen, Oct. 24, 1979.
76. This position was articulated with differing nuances by Köhnen, Kurleman, and Lange, Nov. 1978 and Oct. 1979.
77. Wilhelm Hennis, University of Freiburg, personal conversation, New School for Social Research, New York, April 24, 1978.
78. Edgar Pisani, MEP, interview, Palais de l'Europe, Strasbourg, Nov. 15, 1978.
79. Karlheinz Reif, "European Elections and National Electoral Cycles," (Paper presented at the Annual Meeting of the American Political Science Association, New York, NY, Aug. 31 - Sept. 3, 1978).
80. John Palmer, "French Euro-vote is straw poll,"

146

The Guardian (Manchester-London), May 17, 1979.
81. For an analysis of this point see David White, "Giscard's Men Lead in Opinion Polls," Financial Times, May 22, 1979, and Flora Lewis, "Gaullists Score an 'Unsuccess' as Europe Votes," New York Times, June 17, 1979, sec. 4, p. 3.
82. Simone Veil was subsequently elected President of the European Parliament. See Europe (Sept.-Oct. 1979), pp. 4-6.
83. New York Times, May 11, 1979.
84. Palmer, "French Euro-vote."
85. Le Monde, June 7, 1979 presented a series of interviews with the leaders of the eleven electoral lists.
86. Palmer, "French Euro-vote."
87. The complete lists are available in Le Figaro (Paris), June 7, 1979.
88. See Le Monde Internationale, May 28, 1979.
89. As was noted previously, Jacques Delors and Edgar Pisani campaigned extensively for other Confederation parties.
90. Parti Socialiste, Declaration des Droits des Femmes (Paris: Parti Socialiste, 1978).
91. "French Socialist Leader Resigns from New European Parliament," New York Times, June 21, 1979.
92. Lewis, "Speech by Giscard Heats Political Row," New York Times, April 20, 1979.
93. White, "Giscard's Men Lead," May 22, 1979.
94. ibid.; also see Le Monde, May 17 and 18, 1979.
95. White argues the similarities in issues between the pro-Europe parties in "Giscard's Men Lead."
96. Kurleman, Nov. 15, 1978 discussed this rally's success with great enthusiasm.
97. "Le P.S. fera campagne 'a visage découvert'," Le Monde, May 5, 1979.
98. "Mitterrand a Strasbourg: construire 'l'Europe de gauche'," Le Figaro, May 27, 1979.
99. "M. Mitterrand demande," Le Monde, May 18, 1979.
100. "A l'occasion du 'Printemps de l'Europe' les leaders socialistes des Neuf etaient tous reunis hier a Paris," Le Matin, May 26, 1979.
101. ibid.
102. Pisani, Nov. 15, 1978.
103. European Socialist (April 1979), pp. 10-11.
104. Euro-Report, no. 588, April 11, 1979.
105. "Socialistes francais et britanniques veulent resserrer leurs liens," Le Monde, June 7, 1979.
106. Le Monde, June 6 and 7, 1979, and Le Figaro, June 7, 1979 are prime examples of this reporting. Also see an exclusive interview with Mitterrand in Le Figaro, May 27, 1979.
107. ibid. Also see Le Soir, Le Journal du Centre, and Le Matin, particulary the June 6 and 7, 1979 issues.

108. Parti Socialiste, "Manifeste socialiste pour l'election européenne," Le Poing et la Rose, no. 77 (Oct. 21, 1978), p. 7.

109. Köhnen noted on Oct. 24, 1979 that after the direct elections the PS appointed a liason with functions similar to hers.

110. Europe Press Release, no. 2666, April 25, 1979.

111. Euro-Report, no. 470, Dec. 17, 1977.

112. See, for example, Elinor Goodman, "Labour issues anti-EEC threat," Financial Times, Jan. 25, 1979, and "Mr. Benn aims Labour at the EEC," Guardian, April 9, 1979.

113. Having written to the Labour Party in June 1979 for samples of campaign materials, I received the small leaflet and poster for which the Confederation paid, copies of a few press releases, and a form letter stating that nothing else was produced because "we had no money."

114. Walter Brown, Assistant National Agent, interview, Transport House, London, Nov. 1, 1978.

115. Confidential interview, Strasbourg, Oct. 26, 1979.

116. R.W. Apple, "British Voters Cast a Listless Eye at Europe," New York Times, June 7, 1979.

117. Michael Wood, interview, Palais de l'Europe, Strasbourg, Oct. 24, 1979. Also see Le Monde, June 7. 1979.

118. European Assembly Elections: Manifesto Adopted by the National Executive Committee of the Labour Party (Jan. 1979), and The EEC (1978) are available from Literature Sales, Labour Party, Transport House, Smith Square, London.

119. Barbara Dalzell, "No new market for British goods," Financial Times, June 7, 1979.

120. Francis Wheen and Patrick Wintour, "Roll Up That Map of Europe," New Statesman (June 1, 1979), p. 777.

121. Goodman, "Towering Figure in Tory Campaign," Financial Times, June 7, 1979.

122. "Mr. Benn aims Labour at the EEC."

123. Wheen and Wintour, "Roll Up That Map."

124. "The Need for Euro-voters," Financial Times, May 9, 1979.

125. Michael Wood discussed the Butler and Marquand study on Oct. 24, 1979.

126. Apple, "British Voters Cast Listless Eye."

127. Apple, "European Election Fails to Stir British," New York Times, May 21, 1979.

128. Copies were obtained from the Labour Party, Transport House, London.

129. John Hunt, "Cautious party line on likely turnout in UK," Financial Times, June 7, 1979.

130. See Apple, "British Voters Cast Listless Eye,"

and John Palmer, "Survey Puts UK at Bottom," <u>Guardian</u>, June 8, 1979.

131. Julia Langdon and John Palmer, "Landslide for Tories in Europe," <u>Manchester Guardian Weekly</u>, June 17, 1979.

132. Kurleman, Oct. 24, 1979.

133. This was reported by three confidential sources interviewed in London and Strasbourg. One, a Labour Party activist and pro-Marketeer, had wanted to be a candidate.

134. "Euro-barometer," no. 8.

135. Köhnen, Oct. 24, 1979 contended that it was difficult to make the issues clear to working class people who normally vote socialist, so they simply did not vote.

136. One member of the Socialist Group's Secretariat commented in Oct. 1979 that inexperience was a widespread problem in the new Parliament. However, Labour's single mandate ruling exacerbated this problem for the UK socialists.

137. Ernst Haas, <u>The Uniting of Europe</u> (Stanford: Stanford University Press, 1968), pp. 5 and 15.

5
Neo-Functionalism:
The Missing Element

Neo-functionalist theorists set for themselves a task of historic dimensions: to discover a method of regional political integration which would allow a committed elite of pro-integrationists to bring about the transfer of individual political loyalties to a new regional center while bypassing and not awakening "the sleeping lion of nationalism."[1] Their paradigm has had its greatest test in the European Community which was originally designed according to the neo-functionalist logic. Hence, particular events in the development of political integration within Europe provide opportunities to examine the validity of the neo-functionalist paradigm. The first direct elections to the European Parliament were an occasion for evaluating the crucial dynamic of the neo-functionalist method: spillover.

At the beginning of this study I observed that because the Community method of integration as institutionalized in the Treaty of Rome was prescribed by neo-functionalists, any flaws in the neo-functionalist hypothesis will eventually become evident through studying the Community. I also postulated one mistaken analogy in the neo-functionalist paradigm: the presumption that elites and interest groups will replicate on the European level the political behavior which is successful for them within their national systems, that is, they will attempt to influence those who are the "authoritative allocators of values" in the regional system. My contention was that one set of elites in particular - national political party leaders - will not do so because one vital element is missing: a perception that important decisions at the center of the Community are controllable through organized political power. In short, a lack of democracy in Community decision-making precludes the need for these elites to become involved in Europe. Having studied the activity of three socialist parties before and during the campaign for the first directly elected European Parliament, we will now evaluate this presumption that elites will not replicate

149

national-level political behavior, and discover whether events in 1979 unfolded in a manner a neo-functionalist would expect. In order to do so, the following pages will review the concept of spillover, examine the campaigns of the three parties in light of this concept, evaluate whether integrative behavior which did take place is satisfactorily explained by the neo-functionalist paradigm, and finally come to a conclusion about the neo-functionalist method as a valid means of integrating a regional political system.

THE CAMPAIGN AND NEO-FUNCTIONALIST THEORY

Spillover, as it was discussed in Chapter One, is something that elites unwittingly find themselves doing as they participate in an integration project. Political actors, according to Ernst Haas and Philippe Schmitter, seek to "widen the spectrum of means to influence policy in the evolving regional center," and then they "seek to resolve their problems so as to upgrade common interests, and, in the process, delegate more authority to the center."[2] In other words, national elites, seeing the opportunity to press for certain policy choices at the center, organize themselves in such a way as to win the desired outcomes. If their endeavor is successful, then they are willing to increase the power of the regional government.

There are both horizontal and vertical dimensions to this process of spillover among elites. Horizontally, it becomes necessary for elites in one state to forge links with those in other states who have common concerns, just as it becomes necessary for separate groups to aggregate their interests in order to be effective within a pluralist nation-state. Vertically, the elites find themselves dealing more and more with the new center as they realize there are policies to be influenced there, and these interactions create new ties and establish new patterns of behavior. The European Trades Union Congress (ETUC), for example, has organized itself horizontally among national trade union groupings, and is attempting to forge vertical links with the European bureaucracy in Brussels in order to insure decisions which are favorable to trade unionists.

Early in the history of the European Community, neo-functionalists believed that furthering economic integration would generate spillovers in the political sphere. Haas later reached the conclusion that this was not so, and that economics and politics were autonomous functional contexts insofar as spillover was concerned,[3] that is, economic integration will not have an impact on the political sphere. This seems to have been a valid conclusion because economic decisions in the Community have largely been made by the apolitical Commission, a

situation which is not amenable to pressure from political parties simply because the Commission cannot be
voted out of office by the national parties, and hence
is not subject to their control.[4]
The European Parliament, in contrast to the Commission, is a political body. Its members, until June
1979, were also members of national parliaments, and
they went to Strasbourg or Luxembourg to debate and pass
resolutions on policy matters as is typical of some
functions of a legislative body. The Members of the European Parliament have historically aligned themselves
in transnational political groups and have formed extra-
parliamentary organizations to further the work of
these groups. The Parliament has also been the only
central organ of the Community to face a major structural change in recent years through the 1979 direct election. This situation seemed to be a natural one for
creating significant political activity among national
elites, and for forging new political ties, both vertically and horizontally. There is only one important
problem: this Parliament which represents the major political currents among the Ten has virtually no power.[5]
One must ask, therefore, what an individual political
party had to gain through participation in the direct
elections to the Parliament, and what a party had to
lose by ignoring the event.
The three political parties chosen for this study
have several vague commonalities. They all stem from
the same European socialist tradition, they all belong
to the Socialist International and the Socialist Confederation of the Community, and they all have members in
the Socialist Group of the European Parliament. They
also have substantial divergences which affect their immediate policy decisions. In the United States, the
Democratic parties of Massachusetts and North Carolina,
or the Republican parties of New York and Kansas, also
possess vague commonalities and substantial differences.
However, they fight national campaigns with apparent
unity, and do so for an important reason: a member of
their party in the White House insures a broad range of
rewards. Forging a coalition every four years is well
worth the effort. The reason for this coalition building in the United States - and this is significant -
lies in the democratically controllable power at the
federal level.
Keeping these ideas in mind, we will examine the
European campaigns of the SPD, Parti Socialiste, and
Labour Party in terms of both horizontal and vertical
integrative behavior during the campaign. The SPD ran a
campaign which should have been the pride of any integrationist, and in the course of it loaned top-flight
talent to the Confederation, and took advantage of every
bit of assistance the Confederation was willing to provide. In terms of horizontal linkages, SPD leaders were

at the center of efforts to fight the campaign around one transnational socialist manifesto, and they were active in arranging trading of speakers with parties in other countries. They, as mentioned, went so far in transnational good will as to print one of their major campaign advertisements in French.[6] Not only did the West Germans wage an effective national campaign, they did their best to forge the kind of links which would strengthen social democracy throughout the Community because they saw this as important for their own aims in Europe.[7]

The campaign of the Parti Socialiste was also a serious undertaking in which the leadership worked hard to evoke an internationalist image. Once again, not only was maximum use made of Confederation and Socialist Group resources, but the French did their best to aid the Confederation's efforts, and in fact hosted the major socialist rally of the campaign. They were also "team players" in terms of horizontal cooperation, sending some of their most talented European experts to speak at seminars conducted in other countries.

The British Labour Party was a case apart. The NEC, as has been stated numerous times, refused to deal in any meaningful way with those who were coordinating Confederation efforts, and they certainly did not share the talents of important British political figures with the Confederation. They did absolutely nothing to aid the other socialist parties, and turned down offers of assistance until the very last days of the campaign.

It is important to note that the intransigence of the Labour Party during this campaign has ramifications which extend beyond Labour's defeat in the European election on June 7. On the one hand, as long as they are members of the Socialist Group and the Confederation they can throw blocks in the way of any effort to build enduring transnational links. On the other, it should be noted that those parties which waged campaigns with an integrationist thrust are free to change their positions at any time in the future. There is no compelling necessity to cooperate or be penalized, as the Labour Party has amply demonstrated. This is a distinctly different situation from a national election in which a faction of a party can certainly break away, but knows the penalties might not be worth it.

The French and Germans conducted very "European" campaigns. Was spillover taking place among the members of the PS and SPD, and not among the Labourites? Or were the French and German party elites motivated by possibilities which they well understood and which were by no means mechanistic spillover? This question, whether the process forces expected by neo-functionalism were at work, is of pivotal importance.

The history of the SPD's relationship with the Community, when viewed in isolation, seems to validate the

most optimistic assumptions of the neo-functionalist
paradigm. The Social Democrats were opposed to joining
the Coal and Steel Community in 1952, but immediately
upon entering the Common Assembly they began to play an
activist role. They willingly approved the Treaty of
Rome in 1957, and became even more positive about the
Community after the 1959 Bad Godesberg program was
adopted. Since then the SPD has become a leader of the
Socialist Group, and has also institutionalized communications between its MEPs and its Bundestagfraktion. The
direct election campaign was simply another predictable
step in the SPD's commitment to the idea of uniting
Europe.

Such an analysis neglects politics, and the absence
of an understanding of political power is its critical
flaw. In the early 1950s the SPD was a staunch advocate
of German reunification, and the leading opposition party.[8] Both of these factors made it a political necessity to oppose the ECSC. The SPD's ideological transformation in the middle 1950s, which culminated with the
1959 Bad Godesberg program, allowed the party to view
support for the Community as politically viable. Attempts in the early 1960s to win the allegiance of middle class voters among whom the Community was popular
also required a positive attitude toward the Six. In
the late 1970s the SPD saw an opportunity to influence
the future of Europe of the Nine through maximizing German socialist power in the directly elected Parliament.
The neo-functionalist paradigm cannot explain these political realities. The role of Willy Brandt in the campaign also cannot be explained by neo-functionalism because the theory does not deal with factors such as the
options open or closed to a particular politician.

The Parti Socialiste is a less clear-cut case of
the same type. The French have been critical of the
present Community, yet cooperative within the Socialist
Group. They also spent the 1970s within France attempting to make it clear that they were the major party of
the left, and thus to achieve the presidency of France
in 1981. During much of the 1970s the political goals
of the PS required a tenuous coalition with the PCF.
This coalition forced the PS to downplay its pro-Europe
line because the PCF is bitterly opposed to European integration. At the time of the European Parliamentary
election PS strategy demanded fighting a strong campaign
with Mitterrand at the top of the list. This is not to
say that the PS is not a pro-Europe party with an interest in the Parliament, but rather that French socialist
behavior at the European level is more influenced by national politics than by the unseen hand which guides
spillover.

The SPD and the PS had serious political reasons
for waging highly competitive European campaigns. The
national ambitions of each party required this course of

action. The same assessment holds for the Labour Party,
even though the outcomes are different. For very definite political reasons, some actually based on the historical evolution of the House of Commons, the Labour
Party chose to play down the European election, and to
play up, if anything, the dangers inherent in raising
the profile of the European Parliament. One might disagree with the political wisdom of the route taken by
Labour, but one point is clear: it is impossible to explain the Labour campaign by applying the neo-functionalist paradigm. These three cases lead toward the same
generalization: the reasons why national political parties from the Nine adopted certain policies regarding
the European elections were rooted in their particular
political perceptions at the national level, not in
their gradual involvement in "building Europe."

THE FUTURE OF EUROPEAN POLITICAL
INTEGRATION

     If neo-functionalism cannot account for elite be-
havior during the direct elections campaign, there must
be another explanation for the positive steps toward integration which did take place. I think that explanation lies in the situations discussed above. Party politics at the national level and the short term goals of
individual parties were the deciding factors in planning
European campaigns. Integrative initiatives were certainly taken by some, but not all of Europe's parties.
At least in the cases studied here, there are sound political and ideological reasons to account for these developments.
     The possibility of political gains as the outcome
of integrative behavior seems to be at the root of any
efforts to forge regional political linkages. Regional-
izing policy requires compromise, and political leaders
compromise when a particular goal makes this course of
action worthwhile. A relevant example is the steady
growth of European Political Cooperation. A neo-functionalist might argue that the more the foreign ministers interact the more they become used to it, and this
generates spillovers in the realm of foreign policy making. This reasoning is facile at best. One can find a
much more satisfying answer by observing European response to American efforts to coordinate alliance policy
on, for example, the hostage crisis.[10] The Community
members have found the old cliché, "In unity there is
strength," to be true, and are able, through a common
foreign policy, to overcome what they see as American
attempts to dominate their international affairs. Thus,
real political payoffs provide the impetus for this aspect of political integration. Such concrete gains as a
reward for regional cooperation cannot be realized

through the Parliament at this time.

Two factors about neo-functionalism and the direct elections to the European Parliament have been established: spillover, as explained by neo-functionalists, does not explain the realities of the 1979 campaign; and integrative behavior, where it did exist, can be explained by the national political situations of the parties involved. This analysis, however, leaves a significant question unanswered. If neo-functionalism cannot explain the political integration which does develop, and if the structure of the Community which is designed according to the neo-functionalist model cannot guarantee political integration - as was originally expected - where is the problem in the Community's structure and how can it be corrected?

The problem in terms of integration generated through participation in the Parliament's political groups, the transnational confederations, the new electoral campaigns, and even in terms of national interest groups lobbying any of these groups or confederations, is one of a lack of perceived self-interest. Can a national party afford to commit its best political minds to Strasbourg if little of importance is decided upon, and virtually no decisions are binding?[11] What is the sense of caucussing to the point of obtaining concrete and viable proposals to present to a very weak parliamentary body which cannot legislate? Why compromise on a transnational election manifesto if matters of substance are hardly at stake? And why spend time and money to get your party elected to the Parliament if your MEPs cannot do anything to benefit your constituents?

These questions are particularly germane for anyone, political theorist or European politician, who seeks to create a viable scheme for the political integration of the Community. Even though it is possible that the directly elected Parliament will eventually carve out greater powers for itself, unless these new powers stem from support and interest at the national level they will not push forward the process of building a new political community. This is because the shaping of this community requires changes in actor perceptions about the role of Europe, not just a formal change in that role.

At present there is no good reason for a national party to take the European Parliament seriously. If there is no reason to take the Parliament seriously, then there is no reason to forge the kind of concrete transnational alliances one would need to influence the deliberations of a representative legislature. A power vacuum exists at the center of European Community politics, and it is this lack of democratic control of policy decisions which makes it easy for political parties to resist integration.

My argument now seems to place me on the horns of a

dilemma. I have rejected the neo-functionalist method,
that is, the Community method, as ineffective in foster-
ing significant political integration. However, the
only obvious alternative to uneven gradualism, or possibly stagnation, is an amendment to the Treaty of Rome
granting substantive legislative power to the European
Parliament, that is, a major institutional step toward
federalism. The type of confrontation this would entail
is precisely what neo-functionalists tried to work
around, and rightly so. Political parties who are loath
to participate meaningfully in the present Parliament
would certainly not vote for such amendments when they
came before national parliaments for ratification. Even
most parties from major countries who support the present structure do not approve of federation at this
point.[12] So it would seem that the imperfect, back door
approach of neo-functionalism is the only possible one,
and the probability of a directly elected Parliament
generating political integration of any magnitude is a
long way off. This, however, does not have to be the
case.

    The "Eurocrats", the Community's vast bureaucracy
in Brussels, are supporters of integration.[13] They are
employed by the European Commission as the apolitical
technocrats who are supposed to be the backbone of the
Community. If one remembers that the initial phases of
European integration were in the economic and technical
realms, and that being apolitical was considered a functionalist virtue, it is easy to deduce the bureaucracy's
attitude toward the development of a Parliament with
legislative power.[14] However, these experts and the
Commissioners themselves, who are presumably committed
to a united Europe, could hold the key to political integration generated through the Parliament.

    The Commission and the bureaucracy have the power
to raise the stature of the Parliament. All they have
to do is take its deliberations seriously. They would
have to go through a thought process which first admits
that they want a united Europe, and then a step of ac-
knowledging that they like the technical autonomy the
present Community structure gives them, and then perhaps
draw a conclusion that the two are incompatible. Having
done so, they might decide that their vision of Europe
is their first priority, and that a politically united
Europe cannot be built without politicians. They might
then consider the powerful role they can play simply by
consulting with the Parliament on matters of vital interest to the member states.

    There has been some evidence since the 1979 direct
election that the Commission, in response to pressure
from the Parliament, is taking several tentative steps
in this direction. In fact, reading reports on interaction among the institutions during the early 1980s,
one senses an emerging alliance of Commission and Par-

liament against Council. For example, the Commission has agreed to consult the Parliament on several issues not requiring parliamentary scrutiny according to the Treaty of Rome, and has in fact recommended some small increases in Parliament's role.[15] However, these slight changes are not the stuff of which new political communities are made. They do not have the political potency needed to attract the attention of Europe's parties and voters. What is needed is for the Commission to bypass the Treaty as the Council does in European Political Cooperation, and consult with the Parliament on an issue of major consequence. If the Commission announced its intention to follow such a course of action, and did so before the 1984 direct elections, national parties could not afford to ignore the Parliament.

If the Commission were to choose an issue which generates contention among the Ten, revision of the Common Agricultural Policy (CAP) for example, and announce its intention to work closely and primarily with the European Parliament in every phase of the revision, a ripple effect would most likely appear very quickly. The Labour Party, whose leadership is particularly peeved at the CAP, would become even more peeved at the Tories' dominance of the United Kingdom's eighty one seats and the SPD's hegemony within the Socialist Group. There might even be a British move to bring the Confederation together to work out a common policy regarding the CAP. Interest groups from all over Europe would also descend upon the usually neglected Parliamentarians. By the time the third direct election occurred in 1989, political parties and interest groups throughout Europe would be highly concerned about who would sit in the next European Parliament, and would have to work transnationally for their favored political groups.[16]

If such a scenario were to take place, the technocrats would be aided in their efforts to politicize the Community by forces from among the Ten who favor a strong Parliament. For example, the major West German parties, the political leaders of several of the small countries, and such transnational groups as Agenor (the left socialists who favor integration) would most likely support such new moves with enthusiasm. However, these groups can do little to push the unwilling elites toward integration unless there is a political issue of consequence at stake.

This solution is not entirely a figment of my imagination. While the Commission does not seem quite ready at this time to take such a major step toward reducing its own autonomy, there are indications that the Brussels bureaucracy is as frustrated by the recent stagnation in integration as are many European Parliamentarians. It is ironic that the political strengthening of the Community is most probably in the hands of the technocrats, but that seems to be the case. They alone

can create a situation which can provide the needed perception of self-interest which demands active involvement in the Parliament. They can, through judicious use
of their power, raise the stakes at the level of the European Parliament, and literally force political integration upon the national parties.

CONCLUSION

     This chapter has been brief, but has ranged far
theoretically. It began by reviewing the neo-functionalist concept of spillover, which was supposed to provide the dynamic for political integration. A discussion of horizontal and vertical integrative activities
of three parties participating in the campaign for the
first direct elections to the European Parliament
formed the basis of a conclusion that where integrative
behavior did take place during the campaign it was motivated by national political realities, not by the
spillover dynamic as explicated by neo-functionalists.
Having reasoned that spillover is not going to create
political integration within the present structure, and
that amending the Treaty of Rome is an unworkable idea
at this time, I postulated one way to generate the motivation to work within the European Parliamentary system: a purposive decision on the part of the Commission
and the Brussels bureaucracy to enhance the prestige of
the Parliament by consciously working with it on controversial issues could change the context of European politics.
     This study began by posing several critical ques-
tions about the method of political integration which
has been employed by the European Community since 1958.
The most important of these questions was whether political groups from the member countries would organize
themselves transnationally in order to influence the deliberations of a Parliament which possesses virtually no
power. It was found that individual national parties
may seek to do so if such a course of action enhances
their own political goals, but that parties opposed to
integration can easily block such a project.
     The European Community was formed in 1958 with
great expectations of its ability to transform itself
into a politically united Europe. The methodology of
the project - neo-functionalism - seemed both logical
and exciting. Twenty-five years later the political
goals of the Community's founders have not been realized, and the blame must be placed on the Ten's continued adherence to an unworkable method. The neo-functionalist paradigm, developed from pluralist theory,
seeks to achieve political integration by downplaying
the distinctly political sphere. Neo-functionalism's
missing element is Europe's fatal flaw. If the Commu-

nity is to achieve its goals it will be necessary for the rule of technocrats to be replaced by the debate of politicians. Political power will reside at the center of the Ten when politicians realize that their self-interest demands it. This study of the first European elections has demonstrated that this is not yet the case.

NOTES

1. Gerhard Mally, The European Community in Perspective (Lexington, Mass.: D.C. Heath, Lexington Books, c. 1973), p. 28.
2. Ernst Haas and Philippe Schmitter, "Economics and Differential Patterns of Political Integration," International Organization 18 (Fall 1964): 261.
3. Haas, "International Integration: The European and the Universal Process," International Organization 15 (Summer 1961): 373.
4. The European Parliament has the power to dismiss the entire European Commission, but not an individual Commissioner. See Powers of the European Parliament (London: Information Office of the European Parliament, 1978), pp. 23-26.
5. ibid. This booklet thoroughly outlines all powers and prerogatives of the Parliament.
6. Der Spiegel, June 4, 1979.
7. Helga Köhnen, interview, Oct. 24, 1979 seemed to substantiate this view of the SPD's European ambitions.
8. Carlo Schmid, "Germany and Europe: The German Social Democratic Program," Foreign Affairs 30 (July 1952): 531-534.
9. Labour Party, The EEC and Britian: A Socialist Perspective (London: Labour Party, 1977), p. 66.
10. Flora Lewis, "Europe's Old Complaints on U.S. Policies Have a New Bite," New York Times, sec. 4, March 23, 1980, p. 5.
11. Willy Brandt is supposed to take the Parliament quite seriously, yet he is also the national leader of the SPD, a demanding position. In Oct. 1979 he was present in Strasbourg for one morning of a four day session of the Parliament; personal observation.
12. The French UDF and PS are good examples of this reality.
13. Perhaps the best available study of the Commission and its employees is Altiero Spinelli, The Eurocrats: Conflict and Crisis in the European Community (Baltimore: Johns Hopkins Press, c. 1966). Also consult Philip Taylor, When Europe Speaks with One Voice: The External Relations of the European Community (Westport, Conn.: Greenwood Press, c. 1979) for a good discussion of how the Brussels bureaucracy operates.
14. See EP News, Dec. 1979. This monthly newsletter

is published by the Secretariat of the European Parliament, Luxembourg.

15. For evidence of this trend consult two recent documents prepared by the Commission of the European Communities, "Relations Between the Institutions of the Community," COM (81) 581, final, Oct. 7, 1981, and "The Role of the European Parliament in the Preparation and Conclusion of International Agreements and Accession Treaties," COM (82) 277, final, May 27, 1982. Both are available in the Powers of the European Parliament file (no. 423.02) at the Library of the EC Delegation to the UN, New York.

16. A grant of legislative power could cause realignment among the political groups. Consult Jane P. Sweeney, "Left Alignments in the European Parliament: The Problematic Effects of Integration Theory," Comparative Politics 16 (Jan. 1984).

Bibliography

BOOKS

Adelman, Paul. The Rise of the Labour Party, 1888-1945.
    London: Longman Group Ltd., c. 1972.
Beer, Samuel. British Politics in the Collectivist Age.
    New York: Random House, c. 1969.
Berlau, A. Joseph. The German Social Democratic Party,
    1914-1921. New York: Columbia University Press,
    1949.
Criddle, Byron. Socialists and European Integration: A
    Study of the French Socialist Party. New York:
    Humanities Press, 1969.
Easton, David. The Political System: An Inquiry into the
    State of Political Science. New York: Alfred A.
    Knopf, 1960.
_____. A Systems Analysis of Political Life. New
    York: John Wiley & Sons, c. 1965.
Fitzmaurice, John. The Party Groups in the European Par-
    liament. Lexington, Mass.: Saxon House, Lexington
    Books, c. 1975.
Haas, Ernst B. Beyond the Nation State: Functionalism
    and International Organization. Stanford: Stanford
    University Press, c. 1964.
_____. The Uniting of Europe: Political, Social, and
    Economic Forces, 1950-1957. Stanford: Stanford Uni-
    versity Press, c. 1968.
Henig, Stanley, ed. European Political Parties: A Hand-
    book. New York: Praeger, c. 1969.
Lidtke, Vernon. The Outlawed Party: Social Democracy in
    Germany, 1878-1890. Princeton: Princeton University
    Press, 1966.
Lindberg, Leon. The Political Dynamics of European Eco-
    nomic Integration. Stanford: Stanford University
    Press, c. 1963.
_____ and Stuart Scheingold. Europe's Would-Be Polity.
    Englewood Cliffs: Prentice Hall, 1970.
Mally, Gerhard. The European Community in Perspective.
    Lexington, Mass.: D.C. Heath, Lexington Books,
    c. 1973.

162

Marquand, David and David Butler. European Elections and
    British Politics. London: Longman Group Ltd., c.
    1981.
Noland, Aaron. The Founding of the French Socialist
    Party, 1893-1905. New York: H. Fertig, 1970.
Oudenhove, Guy van. The Political Parties in the Euro-
    pean Parliament. Netherlands: A.W. Sijthoff, 1965.
Pentland, Charles. International Theory and European In-
    tegration. New York: Free Press, c. 1973.
Rousseau, Jean Jacques. The Social Contract. New York:
    Macmillan, Hafner Press, c. 1947.
Schellenger, H. Kent. The SPD in the Bonn Republic: A
    Socialist Party Modernizes. The Hague: Martinus
    Nijhoff, 1968.
Spinelli, Altiero, The Eurocrats: Conflict and Crisis in
    the European Community. C. Grove Haines, trans.
    Baltimore: Johns Hopkins Press, c. 1966.
Taylor, Philip. When Europe Speaks with One Voice: The
    External Relations of the European Community.
    Westport, Conn.: Greenwood Press, c. 1979.

ARTICLES

Agenor. "The Anti-Tindemans Report." Agenor 57 (Dec.
    1975): 3-21.
_____. "Letter to an Anti-Marketeer." Agenor 51
    (Spring 1975): 1-9.
Bell, David S. "The Parti Socialiste in France." Journal
    of Common Market Studies 8 (June 1975): 419-431.
Braunthal, Gerard. "The Political Function of the German
    Social Democratic Party." Comparative Politics 9
    (Jan. 1977): 127-146.
Byrd, Peter. "The Labour Party and the European Commu-
    nity." Journal of Common Market Studies 8 (June
    1975): 469-483.
Charlton, Sue Ellen M. "European Unity and the Politics
    of the French Left." Orbis 19 (Winter 1976): 1448-
    1470.
Crick, Bernard. "The Future of the Labour Government."
    Political Quarterly 38 (Oct. 1967): 375-388.
Crossman. R.H.S. "British Labour Looks at Europe."
    Foreign Affairs 41 (July 1963): 732-743.
Friedrich, Paul. "The SPD and the Politics of Europe:
    From Willy Brandt to Helmut Schmidt." Journal of
    Common Market Studies 8 (June 1975): 432-439.
Haas, Ernst B. "International Integration: The European
    and the Universal Process." International Organiza-
    tion 15 (Summer 1961): 366-392.
_____. "The Study of Regional Integration: Reflec-
    tions on the Joy and Anguish of Pretheorizing."
    International Organization 24 (Fall 1970): 607-646.
_____. "Technocracy. Pluralism, and the New Europe."
    in J.S. Nye, ed., International Regionalism:

Readings. Boston: Little, Brown, & Co., c. 1968, pp. 149-176.

_____. "Turbulent Fields and the Theory of Regional Integration." International Organization 30 (Spring 1976): 173-212.

_____ and Philippe C. Schmitter. "Economics and Differential Patterns of Political Integration: Projections about Unity in Latin America." International Organization 18 (Fall 1964): 705-737.

Herz, John. "Social Democracy vs. Democratic Socialism: An Analysis of SPD Attempts to Develop a Party Doctrine." Paper presented at the Conference on the European Left, City University of New York, Graduate Center, New York, N.Y., Nov. 18-20, 1976.

Jenkins, Peter. "Dilemmas of Social Democracy." Dissent 22 (Fall 1975): 345-350.

_____. "The Future of the Labour Party." Political Quarterly 46 (Oct. 1975): 373-384.

Kaiser, Karl. "The US and the EEC in the Atlantic System: The Problem of Theory." Journal of Common Market Studies 5 (June 1967): 388-425.

Lanx, William. "West German Political Parties and the 1972 Bundestag Election." Western Political Quarterly 26 (Sept. 1973): 507-528.

Lindberg, Leon N. "Decision Making and Integration in the European Community." International Organization 19 (Winter 1965): 56-80.

_____. "The European Community as a Political Community: Notes Toward the Construction of a Model." Journal of Common Market Studies 5 (June 1967): 344-387.

_____. "Integration as a Source of Stress on the European Community System." International Organization 20 (Spring 1966): 233-265.

_____. "Political Integration as a Multidimensional Phenomenon Requiring Multivariate Measurement." International Organization 24 (Fall 1970): 649-731.

Mackintosh, John P. "The Problems of the Labour Party." Political Quarterly 43 (Jan. 1972): 2-18.

Marquand, David. "The Challenge to the Labour Party." Political Quarterly 46 (Oct. 1975): 395-402.

May, James. "Is There a European Socialism?" Journal of Common Market Studies 8 (June 1975): 492-502.

Mitrany, David. "The Prospect of Integration: Federal or Functional." Journal of Common Market Studies 6 (Jan. 1965): 110-149.

Nye, J.S. "Comparing Common Markets: A Revised Neo-functionalist Model." International Organization 24 (Fall 1970): 796-835.

_____. "Patterns and Catalysts in Regional Integration." International Organization 19 (Fall 1965): 796-835.

Palmer, Michael. "The Role of a Directly Elected European Parliament." World Today 33 (April 1977):

122-131.

Pridham, Geoffrey. "Transnational Party Groups in the European Parliament." Journal of Common Market Studies 13 (March 1975): 266-279.

Reif, Karlheinz. "European Elections and National Electoral Cycles." Paper presented at the 1978 Annual Meeting of the American Political Science Association, New York, N.Y., Aug. 31-Sept. 3, 1978.

Rocard, Michel. "French Socialism and Europe." Foreign Affairs 55 (April 1977): 554-560.

Ross, George. "How to Lose an Election: Notes on the French Left." Unpublished manuscript, Brandeis University, Mass., April 1978.

Sahm, Ulrich. "Britain and Europe, 1950." International Affairs 43 (Jan. 1967): 12-23.

Scheingold, Stuart A. "Domestic and International Consequences of Regional Integration." International Organization 24 (Fall 1970): 978-1002.

Schellenger, H. Kent. "The German Social Democratic Party After World War II: The Conservation of Power." Western Political Quarterly 19 (June 1966): 251-265.

Schmid, Carlo. "Germany and Europe: The German Social Democratic Program." Foreign Affairs 30 (July 1952): 531-544.

Schmitter, Philippe. "A Revised Theory of Regional Integration." International Organization 24 (Fall 1970): 836-868.

Sweeney, Jane P. "The Left in Europe's Parliament: The Problematic Effects of Integration Theory." Comparative Politics 16 (Jan. 1984).

_____. "Mitterrand's Economic Program: The Constraints of European Community Membership." Paper presented at the Conference of Europeanists, Washington, D.C., April 30-May 1, 1982.

Taylor, Paul. "The Concept of Community and the European Integration Process." Journal of Common Market Studies 7 (Jan. 1968): 83-101.

_____. "The Functionalist Approach to the Problem of International Order: A Defense." Political Studies 16 (Oct. 1968): 393-409.

Vardys, Stanley. "Germany's Postwar Socialism: Nationalism and Kurt Schumacher." Review of Politics 27 (April 1965): 220-244.

Veen, Hans-Joachim. "The Position of Socialist and Communist Parties and the Integration of Western Europe." Unpublished paper, Konrad Adenauer Stiftung, Bonn, West Germany, 1977.

Wertheimer, Egon. "Portrait of the Labour Party," in Richard Rose, ed., Studies in British Politics: A Reader in Political Sociology (New York: St. Martin's Press, 1966), pp. 34-48.

Wheaton, Michael. "The Labour Party and Europe, 1950-1971," in Ghita Ionescu, ed., The New Politics of

European Integration. New York: St. Martin's Press, 1972, pp. 80-97.

Yergin, Angela Stent. "West Germany's Sudpolitik: Social Democrats and Eurocommunism." Orbis 23 (Spring 1979): 51-72.

EUROPEAN COMMUNITY AND POLITICAL PARTY PUBLICATIONS

Brandt, Willy, "Address to the European Parliament, Nov. 13, 1973." Official Journal of the European Communities: Debates of the European Parliament, English Ed., No. 168, Nov. 1973, pp. 20-25.

Confederation of the Socialist Parties of the European Community. Appeal to the Electorate: Europa '79. Brussels: Confederation of the Socialist Parties of the European Community, 1979.

_____. "Draft Election Manifesto of the Confederation of the Socialist Parties of the European Community." Luxembourg: Confederation of the Socialist Parties of the European Community, 1977.

_____. "European Socialists on the Eve of the Direct Elections." Luxembourg: Confederation of the Socialist Parties of the European Community, 1978.

_____. "Political Declaration of the Party Leaders' Conference, 23-24 June, 1978." Luxembourg: Confederation of the Socialist Parties of the European Community, 1978.

European Community Information Service. European Community News, Washington, D.C., May 15, 1979.

European Parliament. Élections directes: Un Parlement de 410 Sieges. Paris: Parlement Européen, Bureau d'Information, 1978.

_____. European Elections: A Parliament in the Community. Luxembourg: Secretariat of the European Parliament, 1977.

_____. A Parliament for Europe. Luxembourg: Secretariat of the European Parliament, 1978.

_____. Powers of the European Parliament. London: Information Office of the European Parliament, 1978.

_____, Political Affairs Committee, ed., The Case for Elections to the European Parliament by Direct Universal Suffrage: Selected Documents. Luxembourg, Secretariat of the European Parliament, 1969.

European Parliament News. Dec. 10-14, 1979.

European Socialist: Monthly Review of the Socialist Group of the European Parliament. Brussels, June 1978-April 1979.

Goldsborough, James O. "410 Elected in the World's First International Parliamentary Election." Europe. July-Aug. 1979. pp. 6-8.

Hayward, Ron. "Foreward to Appeal to All EEC Electors." London: Labour Party, 1979.

Labour Party. Direct Elections: Arguments for and
Against. London: Labour Party, 1976.
_____. The EEC: Labour Party Campaign Handbook. Lon-
don: Labour Party, 1979.
_____. The EEC and Britain: A Socialist Perspective.
London: Labour Party, 1977.
_____. Labour and the Common Market: Report of a
Special Conference of the Labour Party, 26 April,
1975. London: Labour Party, 1975.
_____. Labour and Europe: Election Communication.
London: Labour Party, 1979.
_____. "Manifesto of the British Labour Party for the
European Assembly Elections." Luxembourg: Confeder-
ation of the Socialist Parties of the European Com-
munity, 1979 (mimeographed).
_____. Speakers' Notes: Euro-Elections - Why Bother?
London: Labour Party, 1979.
_____. Statement to Annual Conference by the National
Executive Committee. London: Labour Party, 1977.
National Referendum Committee. Why You Should Vote No.
London: Her Majesty's Stationery Office, 1975.
New York, N.Y. Delegation of the Commission of the Euro-
pean Communities to the United Nations. Library.
Direct Elections and Socialist Group Files. Europe
Press Releases, 1978-1979. Euro-Report, 1978-1979.
Euro-Barometer, 1978-1979.
Parti Socialiste. Declaration des Droits des Femmes.
Paris: Parti Socialiste, 1978.
_____. "Manifeste Socialiste pour l'élection euro-
péenne." Le Poing et la Rose (Paris). Oct. 21,
1978, pp. 2-7.
_____. "Socialist Manifesto of the French Socialist
Party for the European Elections." Luxembourg: Con-
federation of the Socialist Parties of the European
Community, 1978 (Mimeographed).
Social Democratic Party. Argumente für Europa. Bonn:
Social Democratic Party, 1979.
_____. Dokumente zur Europapolitik. Bonn: SPD, 1978.
_____. Europa Informationen: Quellen zu Otto von
Habsburg. Bonn: SPD, 1979.
_____. Framework of Economic and Political Orienta-
tion of the Social Democratic Party of Germany for
the Years 1975-1985. Diet Simon, trans. Bonn-Bad
Godesberg: Research Institute of the Friedrich
Ebert Foundation, 1976.
_____. Frauen für Europa. Bonn: SPD, 1979.
_____. "Mitteilung für die Presse." Bonn: SPD
Pressedienst, Dec. 11, 1978, March 27, April 27,
May 19, June 8, 1979.
_____. "Programme of the Social Democratic Party of
Germany for the First Direct Elections to the Eu-
ropean Parliament." Luxembourg: Confederation of
the Socialist Parties of the European Community,
1979.

167

_____. Sagt Ja zu Europa. Bonn: SPD, 1979.
_____. Soziale Europa. Bonn: SPD, 1979.
Texts Relating to the European Political Cooperation.
    Bonn: Press and Information Office of the Govern-
    ment of the Federal Republic of Germany, 1977.
Zahn, Paul. "The Advertising Campaigns." Europe.
    July-Aug. 1979, p. 5.

NEWSPAPERS AND PERIODICALS

La Croix (Paris), April 28, 1979.
L'Express (Paris), Oct. 21, 1978.
Le Figaro (Paris), May-June, 1979.
Financial Times (London), Jan.-June, 1979.
Frankfurter Allgemeine Zeitung, June 1979.
Guardian (London, Manchester), Nov. 1978-June 1979.
L'Humanite (Paris), June 26, 1978.
International Herald Tribune (Paris), Nov. 1978-June
    1979.
Manchester Guardian Weekly, Nov. 1978-June 1979.
Le Matin de Paris, April-June, 1979.
Le Monde (Paris), June 1978-June 1979.
Le Monde Diplomatique (Paris), Feb. 1973.
Le Monde Internationale (Paris), May 24, 1979.
New Statesman (London), June 1, 1979.
New York Times, Oct. 1978-June 1979.
Der Spiegel, Jan.-June, 1979.
Times (London), Nov. 8, 1978.
Wall Street Journal (New York), June 12, 1979

Index